LIVING IN THE SHADOW OF GRIEF

ENLARGING YOUR CAPACITY TO GRIEVE WITH HOPE

D6 FAMILY MINISTRY
114 BUSH RD - NASHVILLE, TN 37217 - 800.877.7030 - D6FAMILY.COM

Published by D6 Family Ministry
114 Bush Road
Nashville, TN 37217
d6family.com
ISBN: 9781614842071
Printed in the United States of America

WHAT OTHERS ARE SHARING ABOUT THIS BOOK

Dave and Debbie have endured unimaginable loss and have opened up their hearts and faith for all to see. If you've experienced loss or want to pursue a deeper faith for whatever lies ahead, this is a challenging and hopeful read.

—**Josh Griffin,** *Download Youth Ministry, junior high pastor Mariners Church*

Living in the Shadow of Grief is a sacred gift to anyone walking through the valley of loss. Dave and Debbie Keehn write with authenticity, vulnerability, and deep faith. With each page, they invite readers into their story while pointing them toward the hope only Jesus can give. Their honesty about pain and their unwavering trust in God make this book both comforting and life-giving. Whether you are grieving yourself or walking beside someone who is, you'll find truth, peace, and encouragement on every page. This book beautifully reminds us that even in the shadow of grief, the light of God's grace still shines.

—**Todd Pearage,** *founder and president of The Youth Leader Oasis*

Living in the Shadow of Grief is a raw, gripping, and hopeful book. With the unexpected loss of their young son, Adam, Dave and Debbie had their lives turned completely upside down. There is no perfect formula for grieving. It's messy. And yet, in this book, the Keehns share their heart-wrenching journey of grief and offer biblical principles for grieving with hope.

—**Sean McDowell, Ph.D.,** *professor of Apologetics at Talbot School of Theology, author of over 20 books, and popular YouTuber*

Reading this book has come at just the right time in my own grief journey. At its core, *Living in the Shadow of Grief* radiates with authenticity and vulnerability, graciously allowing its readers permission to grieve and wrestle with the deep, heart-aching questions and feelings that inevitably accompany the grief journey. The words poured out on these pages have been a salve for my own personal pain, inspiring a new way to walk in my own "shadow of grief." This book is a powerful tool, providing deep yet practical insights for navigating grief. Whether you are a ministry leader caring for others, a parent leading your family or you are personally seeking to find your way out of the depths of painful grief, I have no doubt that Dave and Debbie's story will be a beacon of hope in the midst of your journey.

—**Meghan Landi,** *Empowered Homes Ministry*

The valley grief and loss is a constant reality in pastoral ministry. Whether it is our preference for the mountain tops, or our own discomfort seeing ourselves and others in pain, sometimes we can be unaware of this landscape. Dave and Debbie have opened themselves up to chart a course through that valley. This book is practical and biblical guidance for those who find themselves in that valley or are walking with them.

—**Craig Hill,** *senior pastor Taft Ave. Community Church*

CONTENTS

LIVING IN THE SHADOW OF GRIEF:
ENLARGING YOUR CAPACITY TO GRIEVE WITH HOPE

INTRODUCTION

June 8, 2022, changed my life forever.

As a parent I (Dave) never expected to receive that call. As a pastor, it was always another family that had the tragedy, but now it was me. Through tears, my daughter-in-law[1] broke the news: Adam had died. My life has never been the same.

In the months that followed that dark day, my wife, Debbie, and I read some great books on grief (*A Grace Disguised* by Jerry Sittser was especially helpful), but we found there was not a book that looked at the permanent change that grief forced upon us. For twenty-five years, many have encouraged me to write a book, but I never felt I had anything unique to say—until now. I did not want to write this book. I wish I didn't have to. But I write to help those who are hurting to grieve with hope.

This book is for anyone experiencing deep loss, whether it be a cherished loved one, a marriage, or other life-altering change. When our son Adam died, Debbie and I leaned heavily into our faith in Jesus Christ. While you may or may not share this same faith, we hope you will find encouragement in our journey. You will read in the pages ahead of the peace we found in the reality of Heaven according to the Christian Scripture: the Bible. You will witness the difference knowing Jesus as Savior and Lord has made in our lives, but that is not a prerequisite to read this book. We desire to give you an enlarging capacity to grieve with hope, as life will never be the same for you again as well. This book is also for those walking alongside someone on a journey with grief. We hope to give you an understanding that the person you knew before their loss will never be the same again, and to provide you tools to help and not hurt the person further.

The unique insight we offer was gained in our experience of grieving Adam's death. The bottom-line hope we desire to share with you

[1] Throughout this book, we do not give the names of Adam's wife and daughter out of respect for their privacy. This is our (Dave and Debbie's) story of grief, of which they are the unfortunate participants. They would never want any attention from this experience to be focused on them. We wrote our story with their support and we love them dearly.

is that grief evolves, yet never disappears, and, with the grace of God, can actually enlarge our lives. The long shadow of grief is not absent the long arm of God's grace. What do I mean by a "long shadow"?

Have you ever had a feeling you could not shake? Something that shapes how you view your daily experiences? That is how I have felt the past few months; two-plus years now removed from the sudden death of my son, Adam. I've had an insatiable urge to scream into the darkness that envelopes me. This darkness is not depression, but a shadow that touches everything I think, feel, and do. In the shadow, I am able to experience good days. I can laugh with friends. I can enjoy a roller coaster at Disneyland, screaming with glee. I can love my wife and receive her love. I worship God and experience His peace in powerful and personal ways. However, in all of these good moments, I feel the shadow, and it impacts my ability to be fully present in the moment as I move forward in my journey with grief.

I didn't expect the shadow. I did not even know how to name it. It wasn't until now, two years after Adam's passing, that I began trying to figure out what I was experiencing. I started processing with my wife and she nodded and spoke of a similar experience. We both have good days and enjoy the moment. Yet, even as everything was settling in, we began to understand that our new normal was going to be darker than we thought.

This is not a "how to" book, but we will share wisdom we gained along the way. I (Dave) will take the primary lead-author role detailing our journey, explaining the Christian theology of death, suffering, and Heaven; and providing applications to life after loss. Debbie will add her perspective of her journey in ways that differed from me. These paragraphs, a few each chapter, will be identified by a unique handwriting font used. This book is not a substitute for pastoral care or professional counseling, though it has been therapeutic to write and we do hope it comforts and helps. Our aim comes from the words the apostle Paul once wrote to grieving believers in the first century. "But we do not want you to be uninformed, brothers, about those who are asleep [have died], that you may not grieve as others do who have no hope" (1 Thessalonians 4:13, ESV).

Grief is a continued presence in my life because of the love I have for my son. It was not until his death that I considered there were consequences to love. My love for Adam—the value who he is in my life and the impact he's made in the world—perpetuates this feeling of loss in his death. The price of loving someone is the grief you experience in their absence. We hope you receive from reading this book an understanding of how your love is persevering and enlarging your capacity to grieve with hope. This book is written in four sections. The first section of the book seeks to understand how we encounter grief and the full weight of its impact. The second section of the book offers some pathways (not advice) that helped us to respond to the deep grief of losing our son. The last two sections of the book are meant to understand pieces of your brokenness that are your "new normal," and how to live with these new characteristics as instruments of hope.

Grief is like a ball in a jar. The ball does not get smaller over time, but rather what I am finding is while the ball of grief may remain the same size, the jar is enlarging—enlarging my capacity to grieve with hope. By God's grace, I am able to care more for others. I am able to give more to my family. I am able to take on more opportunities for the sake of God's kingdom work. I have found that, through the grace of God, I am enlarging as a person: my preaching has more substance, my compassion is more authentic, my purpose more focused. My grief is not a hindrance to this growth, but, by the wisdom and mercy of God, my grief grows me. Our prayer is that your journey in the grief will be with hope—not in the past life returning, but that the new normal you are living in, the shadow of grief will become the backdrop to a beautiful life that God is enlarging you to become.

CHAPTER 1
THE LAST WORD

ADAM'S STORY

A friend wrote me an email when he learned that my son, Adam, had suddenly died. He proclaimed over the situation: "Jesus has the last word and won't let Adam's story end here." I have lived with that truth squarely in front of me, guiding me, sustaining me in this long journey with grief. Adam's story did not end that dreadful day on earth.

But how did Adam's story begin?

Adam almost wasn't. Debbie got very sick after the birth of our first child, Aimee. According to the medical advice we received, we should not get pregnant because of the very powerful medication that was keeping her system alive. I was angry at God. We got married young and were able to conceive Aimee quickly—she was born almost on our second wedding anniversary. The honeymoon was over, and the vows of our marriage were tested: for better, for worse; in sickness and in health. God reminded me of these vows one night as I railed against Him. Almost three years later, Debbie's health improved, and the doctors gave us permission to try again to conceive a child. Debbie stopped taking the medication and we were soon pregnant again. However, Debbie's health quickly declined again, forcing her back on the dangerous medication. We were barely through the first trimester, but we could not wait any longer; prayerfully Debbie was hooked up to an IV and bedridden for most of the remainder of the pregnancy.

Debbie's "water" broke just after midnight on Sunday, September 7, 1997. We went to the hospital to begin the arduous journey that is childbirth. Our church, where I was serving as the youth pastor, announced in the worship services that we were at the hospital as part of their prayer time—numerous people got up and left to join in the hospital wanting to support us in the moment. Later that day Adam was born. However, he was immediately in distress. Instead of placing Adam on Debbie's chest, as most babies are, they whisked Adam out of the room and down the hallway. Debbie, sensing something was wrong, yelled for me to follow Adam. When I found my son, he was blue. The doctors and nurses were hovering around him, giving him oxygen and trying to stimulate his body to respond on its own. Finally, I heard the sound I had been waiting for—Adam's first cry. His screaming was miraculous. Adam was alive and doing well!

Adam was our miracle child, and we knew he was a gift from God right away. Because of Debbie's ongoing medical condition, she couldn't nurse Adam. This meant I got to take some of the night shifts, getting a bottle ready and feeding Adam. Those hours in the dark, feeding Adam, gave me time to pray over him—praying for God's blessing and will to be done. Debbie and I truly believed God gave us Adam for a reason; we were just waiting to discover what he would become. I prayed Psalm 139:16 over him: "Your eyes saw my unformed body; all the days ordained for me were written in your book before one of them came to be" (NIV). I dreamed what all those days would be, never did I think I would see the fullness of those days.

Adam was an active child. He loved to climb, run, and play hard like most young boys. Debbie and I knew we needed to find an outlet for all that energy. We tried multiple youth sports programs. First up was baseball. Adam was small but very fast. He was an ideal lead-off hitter for the coach. Adam did not like this situation; he did not enjoy all the attention with everyone yelling his name in encouragement as he would be the first batter for our team. Adam also found baseball too slow as he often played defense in the outfield to chase down the ball. Standing around for something to happen was not Adam's way of doing life—I observed this early on. So, after a few seasons, we moved onto basketball. Adam enjoyed the running up and down the court, but his short stature made it difficult for him to shoot the ball. Basketball did not last long in our schedule. Adam was invited to join a youth soccer team with his friend, and he found his promised land. Adam's quickness was an asset on the large soccer field. Adam was one of 22 boys on the field so even if I yelled his name, he did not focus on it. Adam grew in his soccer skills quickly and was invited to join a new club team, with a new coach.

Adam loved soccer. Adam thrived in this environment. The friends made and instruction for life that he received in this young season of life were foundational to the man he would become. The loyalty Adam displayed was formed on the soccer team—loyal to a coach and teammates when he was offered opportunities to move to teams with greater prestige. The hard work and sacrifice that Adam demonstrated in his ministry leadership were from the hours of practice and drilling that were done when no one was watching. Adam loved people as they were; he was gracious with his teammates when they were lacking in skill. Adam saw the benefit of leading his peers on the soccer team, receiving honors from his coaches, and his impact on forming a team-first mentality.

Adam's passion for soccer led him to play competitively through high school. Adam stopped playing at the club level when he entered Biola University, opting instead to play intramurals with his friends. He gathered around himself like-minded college students, those who played soccer in high school with skill but did not want to continue at the collegiate level. Adam formed a team of these highly skilled players and they won the whole league his freshman year. However, after that first year Adam decided to focus on other priorities.

Looking back on Adam's journey, it cannot be understated that Adam grew up in a pastor's family, which meant Adam had to go to church. This became a source of struggle for Adam when he was in high school. Adam wrestled with his faith, trying to adjust to the lifestyle he saw his friends enjoying. I believe Adam had a faith in "God," but he had not surrendered his life to Jesus yet. During Adam's teenage years he saw his relationship with God enmeshed in his relationship with his parents. Adam and I struggled to find common ground to build our relationship upon. In desperation, I turned to soccer. Adam and I got season tickets to the Los Angeles Galaxy soccer games. During the long drive to and from the stadium, I would try to talk to Adam about life and Jesus, but he would simply fall asleep on me. Debbie and I continued to pray, and I was constant in my love for Adam. To accommodate Adam's desire to advance in his soccer "career," we enrolled Adam in JSerra Catholic High School in San Juan Capistrano, as they had a high-level athletic program and a ranked soccer program with a coach brought in from Europe. For the first time Adam was being taught something different about Jesus than he had heard from me. His Bible classes held onto many of the key truths Adam learned in Sunday School, but the application and practices of following Jesus were different. Adam would come home from school and ask me questions about God. When Adam was a sophomore in high school, he went to Costa Rica with me for a mission trip. This trip provided opportunities for me to press into what he believed about Jesus. I was still hitting a wall when it came to surrendering life to Jesus, but God was working on Adam's life.

Over the next few years, we experienced new lows and more challenging circumstances with Adam's behavior. When I thought Adam was walking away from God once and for all, Adam had an experience with the Holy Spirit at a senior retreat with his school. God revealed to Adam in a vision of two paths ahead of him; he saw people he knew from our church ministry—Adam took this as a call to return to what he knew from a child to be true. That encounter led Adam to decline pursuing playing soccer in college and enter Biola University, still unsure of what Jesus was asking of him. In God's providence, Adam was surrounded in his dorm that freshman year with many God-fearing Jesus followers who ministered graciously to Adam. Adam sensed the love of God and for the first time in his life understood the grace of Jesus. Adam in his first year at Biola had his "coming to Jesus" moment and fully surrendered his life to Jesus.

As Adam deepened his faith in Jesus, he got involved in sharing the grace of Jesus with others. During the Christmas break of his sophomore year at Biola, Adam participated in a mission trip to do street witnessing in Chicago and work with local churches' holiday outreach. I was impressed with his desire to do this but questioned the methodology of the mission. I told him, "Adam—no one is on the streets of Chicago in December; it's -4 degrees!" Unfazed, Adam simply responded, "We will find them and share Jesus still." That's exactly what Adam did—Adam shared Jesus!

When he returned to school for the spring semester, I met Adam in the café at Biola to talk about next steps for his life, pressing him to consider the career he would pursue. Basically, I told him that he needed to get a job. I was eating in the café that day because I was hosting dozens of local youth pastors on Biola's campus for a day of meetings. During our lunch, the middle school pastor at Mariners Church Irvine, Justin Herman, walked up to Adam noticing the sleeves of tattoos that Adam has, and says to Adam, not knowing Adam is my son, "Dude, I like your ink—I want you to come work for me." Adam turns to me and says, "Look dad, I got a job!" I pointed out that Justin was offering an unpaid summer internship, but Adam took that opportunity on with the same passion, energy, and effort he gave to the soccer field. God worked in and through Adam that summer. When it was time to return for his junior year, Adam declared God was calling him to be a youth pastor, switched into the ministry major at Biola in which I taught, and joined the paid staff at Mariners as the part-time weekend coordinator for middle school.

It was amazing to watch Adam serve his middle school students in various ministry contexts. Debbie and I would sneak up on Saturday nights to watch Adam teach a Bible study and share the gospel of Jesus with hundreds of middle school students at Mariners. I was so proud to tour the youth offices where he had theology books on his desk. Adam loved his students dearly and they loved him back. He was a pied piper for Jesus. During Adam's senior year at Biola, his time at Mariners finished but he quickly began to interview for youth pastor positions across Southern California. Through a brief encounter I had with the executive pastor at Grace Church Glendora, Adam met, interviewed, and was hired as the middle school pastor for this church in February 2020. The next month COVID shut the world down.

However, because Adam was so passionate for the gospel and innovative with technology, his ministry continued and even grew during this "lockdown" season. Adam preached online, "Doordashed" food to students so they could have a virtual lunch together. Adam met students where he could, even on their driveways, encouraging them to carry on in the depressing era COVID became. When his ministry could return to meeting together outside, it had actually grown in size and commitments to Christ during the COVID pandemic. I sat back in amazement again, marveling at the work of God in Adam's life.

Relationally, Adam was thriving with family and friends. After his "coming to Jesus" moment in his freshman year at Biola, Adam and I reconciled the brokenness of his tumultuous teenage years. In the next six years before his death, Adam and I became best friends, as we sought each other for fun and advice. His relationship with the rest of his family improved as well. It was also during this time that Adam met his wife at Mariners Church where she volunteered in his ministry. Adam was smitten by her quickly and we watched their relationship blossom into marriage. The full-time job at Grace Church gave Adam the resources to get married and he had a small wedding in the church's courtyard the November (2020) after he was hired. Adam and his wife loved to do ministry together; she was the anchor his creativity and energy needed to stay grounded in the work God had called him to do. They wanted a family, so after getting a dog, Adam's wife became pregnant. Adam was excited to become a father, talking to and praying for his unborn child. Adam was three weeks from meeting his daughter when the worst became our reality.

Adam was missing from his staff meeting. His boss felt something was wrong and reached out to Adam's wife, who was at work and missed these phone calls. Eventually around noon, Adam's wife got the messages and rushed home to find Adam unresponsive. An autopsy later would reveal Adam suffered a massive brain aneurysm and died instantly. Nothing could have been done to save him.

I was riding along with Orange County Fire truck 59 and just finished an emergency medical call in the community where I live, when I got the call from Adam's wife. When she said, "I think Adam died," I told her to call 911 and we will be right there. In my mind, Adam had a seizure, a stroke, something that required medical attention and he would be alright again. Adam's wife was telling me the truth, but I could not accept it yet. I called Debbie who was shopping at the time, "Something has happened to Adam—come home now!" I was not sure what happened, but I was not thinking death—I couldn't entertain that thought. The fire truck took me back to the station running their lights and sirens to get me there as quickly as possible. When Debbie and I were able to meet at our house we got another phone call, this time from Adam's wife's sister—I could hear wailing in the background and she confirmed the worst, "He's gone." Now it was time for us to cry out in pain. As a chaplain for the local fire department, I comforted countless parents in their darkest moments of grief. Now, people were coming to me, and I did not want their comfort. I was in shock and disbelief. I was numb to the world. It was not until the next morning that I broke. I cried. I sobbed. I screamed.

A family friend passed our story on to other churches for prayer and somehow our tragic news found its way to the well-respected pastor, Greg Laurie. He too had experienced the loss of a son; he got my phone number and called me. As he talked, I listened to his story, to his challenges of leading amidst the grief and to his warning counsel: "your life has forever changed." Greg was right. I am not the same person. My "normal" is different. Death changes things we experience in life.

One of the last Bible studies Adam taught his students is "Jesus changes everything." We found stickers and graphic designs in his office with this proclamation that we have since made into t-shirts as well. When we wear this t-shirt in public, testifying the reality that Jesus does change everything, we get stopped by people to affirm that truth. Death may have changed some things in my life, but Jesus has the power to change everything! Jesus even changed how I think of death and its finality.

When the perishable has been clothed with the imperishable, and the mortal with immortality, then the saying that is written will come true: *"Death has been swallowed up in victory."*

"Where, O death, is your victory?

Where, O death, is your sting?"

The sting of death is sin, and the power of sin is the law. But thanks be to God! He gives us the victory through our Lord Jesus Christ (1 Corinthians 15:54–57, NIV).

I reflect often on my friend's email message, "Jesus has the last word and won't let Adam's story end here." *It is the hope I live by!* Jesus' last word from the cross, "It is finished" (John 19:30), means that my life could begin. Jesus' last word over creation will cause every knee to bow before Him in recognition that He is God (Philippians 2:9–11). Jesus' last word about Adam's earthly life was His first words to Adam in Heaven, "Well done, good and faithful servant! … Come and share your master's happiness" (Matthew 25:21). "Jesus has the final say" produces the hope of eternal life, which makes life on earth meaningful but the ultimate purpose for living; there is something, therefore, much greater to live for.

Adam lived that way too. Paul affirmed the Colossian church in his epistle, stating,

We always thank God, the Father of our Lord Jesus Christ, when we pray for you, because we have heard of your faith in Christ Jesus and of the love you have for all God's people—the faith and love that spring from the hope stored up for you in heaven and about which you have already heard in the true message of the gospel (Colossians 1:3–5, NIV).

Adam had an amazing faith in what God alone would do. Adam loved all people—just as they were. I believe he lived this way because when he trusted Christ as Savior and Lord, the reality of Heaven was his hope. I want to be known that way too. What is such a loss to me is equally a gain for Adam. He is living in the presence of Jesus—his hope fulfilled. Adam is fully alive but I am broken-hearted as I await to be reunited with my son.

I'm not alone in experiencing loss and feeling broken-hearted in the death of loved ones. The apostle Paul wrote to a suffering church about the truth of Christ-followers' experience with death, loss, and grief. "But we do not want you to be uninformed, brothers, about those who are asleep [have died], *that you may not grieve as others do who have no hope*" (1 Thessalonians 4:13, emphasis added, ESV). Our grieving with hope is not wishful thinking. Our questions about the afterlife may cause fear but Jesus responded to this very issue when he was talking with His disciples at the Last Supper. In one of His last words to His best friends and followers He comforted them with these words:

> *Let not your hearts be troubled. Believe in God; believe also in me. In my Father's house are many rooms. If it were not so, would I have told you that I go to prepare a place for you? And if I go and prepare a place for you, I will come again and will take you to myself, that where I am you may be also* (John 14:1–3, ESV).

Jesus' words contained a description of where we will be after death. When Jesus described this place, He deliberately chose common, physical terms (house, rooms, place) to describe where He was going and what He was preparing for us—this is our first clue to what Heaven will be like. Heaven is a real, tangible place and able to be experienced in ways we know today. We can grieve with hope because of the reality of Heaven. We grieve with hope because we will be reunited in resurrection with our Savior and our loved ones. We grieve with hope because "Jesus has the final say." Jesus has the last word!

Jesus' last word is Adam's first work. Adam is living and active in Heaven. I picture Adam, energetically welcoming those who have died after he did—his papa and abuela, and other friends who have died. As his father, I know I will see Adam again—the Adam I know and remember as the passionate young man, full of life. This is not just my hope; this is a statement of faith.

As you read this book, you may not be able to claim the faith Adam had. For some, the grief you feel is too much to process still. My hope is each of the following stages Debbie and I had to work through and process over years and tears will become a pathway for you in your journey with grief. Ultimately, to all who read this book, may the truth that Jesus has the last word, be both a caution and the ultimate hope for you. Live in the shadow of grief as this is not the end of your story.

SECTION 1

ENCOUNTERING GRIEF

For some of you, grief is an "old acquaintance." You have dealt with loss on multiple levels, many times. However, each loss is different and will cause you to grieve differently. This section is meant to help you reconsider the most recent encounter with grief, desiring to give you an expanding capacity to grieve with hope. To the rest of you, grief is an unwelcomed addition to your life. You were not expecting the loss, you are not ready to grieve as deeply as you are. For you, this section is meant to give you some basic understanding of the chaos you are now experiencing, providing you a lifeline of hope.

CHAPTER 2
THE SUDDENNESS OF GRIEF

If I am honest, June 7, 2022, was one of the best days of my life. We were celebrating my wife's birthday at Disneyland with our daughter Aimee, her husband and our granddaughter, and our youngest son Mfundo. I bought a Father's Day shirt for Adam as he would soon be welcoming his first child with his wife. I remember a distinct feeling of God's graciousness and blessing. It's head-spinning how fast you can go from the highest of highs to the lowest of lows.

Some storms come with warnings, earthquakes do not. When an earthquake hits, even small ones, there's a moment where you stand frozen; the ground moves but you do not. You're trying to understand what is happening. Losing a loved one is similar in many ways. It's sudden. It's disorienting. We have no chance to prepare ourselves for what is to come. We don't get to say goodbye. We are frozen. We are confused, not able to fully understand what just happened. In an instant, our lives as we know them come to a sudden and painful end. We can't even begin to think of what the new life will be.

The last time I saw Adam was a great day. He came down with his truck to help me with some errands. In return, I treated him to lunch and a movie. I have fond memories of that pizza lunch and the Marvel movie. When we said goodbye, we hugged each other and drove off in separate directions. I could see his truck turn onto the freeway. It reminded me of the last scene in the movie "Furious 7," of the Fast and Furious franchise, when Paul Walker's character drives off as a loving honor to the actor who passed away during the filming of the movie. Looking back, it was an ominous impression that still haunts me. We were supposed to see Adam and his wife in a week to celebrate Father's Day and then a few weeks later we expected the birth of his daughter. I did not expect what came instead. I was not prepared, nor could I have been.

Even those who grieve the death of a loved one after a long-term illness experience the suddenness when death finally comes. Even then, we don't know when that final breath will come. While there may be relief that someone's physical suffering on earth has ended, there is still a suddenness of the new reality we find ourselves in. My dad fought cancer for two long years of prolonged deterioration, but even then, I did not expect the phone call with the news he'd passed. I rejoiced that my dad was in Heaven enjoying new life, but the fact that I would never sit beside his hospital bed again was suddenly thrust upon me.

Debbie's Journey

My last memory of Adam was the same day he came over to help his dad with his errands. He was leaving our home with Dave to go to lunch and a movie, and I gave him a big hug and kiss. The high of celebrating my birthday and anticipation of celebrating my son becoming a father felt like all was right where it should be. I don't freeze in an earthquake like some do, I react and get loud. On that day, June 8, when we received the call, I began to wail and cry out in the deepest pain and despair. At the same time, I felt the presence of Jesus, and I felt my heart and guts were removed from my body. His presence led me to cry out to Him in my pain!

The fragility of life brings about a fear that the suddenness of grief confirms. We may say, "Any day I wake up is a good day" or "we don't know how much time we have on earth"—but most of us live as if we are invincible. We never think of death, especially the young people among us. Therefore, when death unexpectedly comes, the suddenness of grief is an earthquake to our soul, our relationships, our wellbeing, and our life.

THE SUDDENNESS OF GRIEF AND ITS IMPACT

Grief is an intense emotional reaction to loss. I've always heard of grief coming in stages: denial, bargaining, anger, depression, and finally acceptance. Psychiatrist Elisabeth Kübler-Ross in her 1969 book, *On Death and Dying*, developed this model from interviews with terminally ill patients coming to terms with their own impending death, not to describe the process of grieving the death of a loved. Missing from this sequence in grieving death is the ability to truly "bargain" as I will never see Adam again this side of Heaven. However, I found I was still bombarded by the various feelings, all at the same time. I ricochetted against my overwhelming sadness, to denial, to a moment of acceptance, right back to sadness, then to anger, and round and round it went. I was the pinball in the machine. In the suddenness of grief, we are consumed with sadness as the emotional expression of our denial that the worst has occurred. We sit in the sadness reflecting all we have lost in the passing of our loved one. The primary role the loved one played in your life will be the first loss that you grieve. When a spouse passes away, the widow has lost their lover, companion, friend. When a parent passes away, the child has lost their protector and role model. When a child passes away, the parent has lost "what might have been"—all the potential happenings that will no longer be.

THE IMPACT OF PRIMARY LOSS

In the suddenness of grief, these primary losses create deep sadness. The physical reactions, which adds stress to grief, are often unseen so perhaps it is best to consider grief to be an iceberg. As with an iceberg, we only see a small fraction of what is really there. Using this analogy, the expressions of grief we see are the crying at a funeral, the absence of engagement in normal daily routines. However, "under the waterline," what we don't see, is all the stresses grief is causing: the tightness of the chest, the feeling you can't breathe, feeling isolated, the feeling of guilt that perhaps more could have been done, the sleepless nights, the lump in your throat that never goes away. These are just some of the physical reactions to the suddenness of grief as you begin to realize how life has changed.

THE IMPACT OF SECONDARY LOSS

The completeness of this life change is due also to the secondary losses, which create paralyzing fear within us. Secondary losses are what the loved one gave us besides their presence. Things that impact our ongoing life. Like the widow who loses her primary financial provider, she loses more than just an income. Other secondary losses of a spouse could include:

- Loss of identity
- Loss of support system
- Loss of long-term financial security
- Loss of intimacy
- Loss of confidence
- Loss of faith
- Loss of parenting partner
- Loss of dreams for the future

The list could go on. Death has stolen what could have been later and what is necessary now. This loss of stability creates stress that cripples us, especially when combined with sadness of our loved one's absence. On the Holmes and Rahe stress scale, the death of a spouse is 100 points.[2] All these secondary losses increase that number, making us prime candidates for illness and mental health breakdowns.

No one realizes how much they lost when their grief begins. It evolves over time. Your first thoughts may be, "How will I make it?," referring to some of these secondary losses. Other losses will become much more apparent as the days go on. This prolongs our sadness and makes working through the grief difficult because it feels like each new realization thrusts you back to the beginning. The sudden-

---

[2] The American Institute of Stress, "The Holmes-Rahe Life Stress Inventory," Stress.org, accessed October 1, 2025, https://www.stress.org/wp-content/uploads/2024/02/Holmes-Rahe-Stress-inventory.pdf.

ness of grief is like the amputating of a limb; you no longer have the use of it, and it takes a lot of time to learn how to live without it. The suddenness of grief is also like a wave on the beach that crashes on the sandcastle you were building; what is left behind looks nothing like the structure you had been working. So, how do we live without them?

HOW TO LIVE AFTER THE LOSS IN THE SUDDENNESS OF GRIEF

BREATHE

Just try to breathe. When that terrible news comes, your breath will be stolen from you. There will be tightness in your chest. Your mind is so consumed trying to understand the unthinkable that it forgets to tell your lungs to breathe. So, breathe—slowly—intentionally. Breathe. There is more to do than just breathe, but my purpose is to help you survive this moment, and to do that you must start with breathing.

PRAY

I want to encourage you to focus your mind in these first moments of loss by saying "Breath Prayers." These are short prayers that you can say in one breath. "God help me." "God save me." "Jesus!" These prayers will help with two things. First, they'll make sure that your breathing is steady and deliberate. Second, they'll focus your eyes on God. Only with your eyes set on Him will you begin to find the right posture of dependence you will need in the coming days, weeks, months, and years.

EMBRACE

You probably found yourself wailing and screaming, Debbie did, and this normal emotional response to sudden grief is understandable. However, this emotional response can also lead to hyperventilation (breathing too much). When a wave hits the sand, it is called a "shore breaker" and the impact is as devastating as it sounds. When grieving suddenly, this is the extreme emotional wave that you must endure and then prepare for many more to come. Therefore, as the first emotional wave begins to recede, you must begin to change your posture to one of embrace. Embrace is not acceptance, at least not yet, but readying yourself for what is inevitable and out of your control. This is where Breath Prayers can help you steel yourself to endure the continued waves of grief as you realize the full brunt of the loss.

REACH OUT

Have you noticed that when little children play in the ocean waves, they are holding onto someone else. They know the waves are too much for them to handle on their own. The suddenness of grief must be handled the same way—reach out to someone. The most instinctive movement when you hear tragic news is to collapse; the body cannot handle the emotional weight of what it just heard. The second instinctive body movement is reach for someone else. You grab their shoulder; throw your arms around someone; reach for a hand. Even if you do not want to be touched, and that is ok if you don't, you will need others to emotionally lift you up. Who will you reach out to in that moment?

For many people, family members will be the primary source of emotional strength we will rely on. However, due to current society norms, many of us do not live close to family and you will need someone who can be at your side quickly. Debbie and I called Jake and Shelli in that terrible moment. We call them our "five-minute friends." The reason for that name is these are friends who will drop everything and get to us within five minutes. When we told them the news of Adam's passing, Jake and Shelli came immediately over to the house. Shelli hugged Debbie and did not let her go. I was in shock and could not receive the physical support Jake was offering but he began to care for me in other tangible ways. Jake and Shelli drove us the hour's distance to where Adam was. The whole time all I could do was silently say breath prayers. Jake made sure I had water to drink. Jake and Shelli stayed with us, by our side, for the rest of that day and night. They had plans, but they cleared their calendar to be physically with us in those first sudden moments of grief.

Who are your "five-minute friends"? Who did you reach out to? If you are reading this and cannot name someone other than your immediate family members who would be your "five-minute friends," I would strongly encourage you to invest time to develop those types of friendships. There will be other people who can help you in the moments of grief: people from your church, a sports team you play with, neighbors who live close by. These people may not be relationally close enough to be able to drop everything to be with you, but they can be present with you over the next season of life. You are the one who will decide what parts of the journey with grief you will allow other people to be with you. However, you may realize the hard way that many people are not ready or able to be present with someone in intense grief and will withdraw rather than seek to comfort. Invest time now into various relationships to increase your network of support, because when the next wave of tragedy crashes into you, you will need someone to hold you up.

CONSIDER WHAT YOUR LIFE'S FOUNDATION IS BUILT UPON

After a severe storm has passed, television cameras record and share the totality of devastation caused. Broken trees, damaged houses, displaced lives. All those descriptions could apply to your life when you lose a loved one. When you survey the devastation, it feels like everything is destroyed. Jesus tells a story of a severe storm in Matthew 7. The story is about a storm that impacts two different men in two different ways. The "foolish man" who has built his house down in the riverbed, on a foundation of sand, had his house destroyed in the flood waters. However, Jesus says of the "wise man" who had built his house higher up on the rock, "the rain came down, the streams rose, and the winds blew and beat against that house; yet it did not fall, because it had its foundation on the rock" (Matthew 7:25, NIV). In my naivety, I used to think the wise man's house escaped all damage, however after the passing of Adam, I have a different perspective. The storm was severe. The rain pelted. The winds beat. The house stood because of its foundation, but there was no doubt damage was done to the house. I can now picture the roof may need to be repaired; the windows have been blown out. In the tragedies of life, you too will observe damage, but the house—your life—can still stand because the foundation is solid!

The point of Jesus' story is to consider what are you building your life's foundation on. Those who practice the teachings of Jesus in their daily lives have built their foundation on a solid rock. Notice the foundation is comprised of what you do now in your daily life: the spiritual routines of Bible reading and prayer, the friends you are invested in, and the spiritual community you gather with. Debbie and I practiced these spiritual habits before Adam's passing, and we continued these spiritual practices daily after Adam's passing. Our foundation was built on the solid rock of Jesus. You will read throughout this journey in the shadow of grief that our lives being dependent upon Jesus is a constant theme. Grief has challenged our faith; that is why I say the house, though built on a solid foundation, now has damage to deal with. Debbie and I have had our faith in God tested and we came through this tragedy still believing God is good and loving, but not always gentle with us and He did not promise to make life fair. The suddenness of grief challenges us to surrender to the sovereignty of God, however I will save that discussion for a later chapter. For now, please know God is the one who is with you and was with you when the suddenness of grief came crashing upon you.

FOR THOSE WALKING ALONGSIDE THOSE WHO ARE GRIEVING

Some of you are reading this book to help others through tragedy. Here are a few practical ways to love them well through the beginning phases of the shadow of grief.

GRIEVE

When someone you care for suddenly experiences a traumatic loss, your natural first reaction will be to respond with an urgency to *do* something to help. It is a good and compassionate response, but it may not be the best action. Instead, grieve with them. This loss has "sucker punched" you too. This loss has taken you by surprise and you need to grieve as well. What is worse about your situation is the pressure you put upon yourself to help alleviate the pain of the situation. When Adam passed away, many people were overwhelmed with grief: the youth of Adam's ministry and his church, the churches where I had served and was serving at the time, his soccer team, his college roommates, and our large extended family. All these groups felt a need to help, but it became overwhelming as they all contacted me at once. We must be careful not to overwhelm the person who has lost a loved one. The best help we received were simply the long, silent hugs from people who were grieving too. We did not need a lot of words, although some well-timed and thoughtful texts and emails were especially encouraging. The best thing about those texts and emails is I could go back on my own and re-read them. In each of these examples, the people allowed their grief to guide their response to us.

WAIT

For those walking alongside someone suddenly grieving, the best response to the suddenness of grief is to wait, wait for the other person to initiate the hug, to initiate the conversation. Be present but be silent. Be present but wait in prayer. How grateful I am as well for those in the initial days who simply prayed for us. I was sent a picture from our church on the night Adam died; it was simply a scene of fifty-plus people who spontaneously gathered at our church to pray for our family. I don't know who or how this prayer time was organized but that was the best response my church could give us. Be visible and available, but wait for the person grieving, to reach out to you.

Debbie's Journey

Many have good intentions. In those good intentions, some shared their own past experiences with grief; they wanted me to know that they too know my loss. Those good intentions are not necessarily wrong, but they resulted in words shared that were in poor taste and very bad timing. Please don't share your own story of grief with the one who is grieving and in pain. I only share this out of experience. I have learned many lessons of what not to do and say with someone in the deep pain of loss. I have also learned that for someone like me, the journey in grief and the processing of pain can take a bit longer to reemerge back into public. I needed longer than Dave to stay away from groups of people than he did, and that worked best for me. Everyone's journey with grief is different and therefore don't feel like you know someone else's journey.

CARE FOR PHYSICAL NEEDS

If you must do something, focus on the physical needs that are present. A simple example is to organize meals for the family. I got the news of Adam's passing right before lunchtime and our family did not feel like eating for hours, but late in the afternoon, when I finally felt a twinge of hunger, food was there—easy to eat food, finger sandwiches, fruit, and lots of cold-water bottles. This was a gracious gift of love. Churches organized "meal trains" but the best meals were gift cards to Door Dash and Grubhub, which allowed my family to order what we wanted, when we wanted it. A well-organized "meal train" will have one person as the main contact and will leave a food cooler outside the house for people to place the meals in. This allowed us to maintain privacy and receive a phone text message from the one contact person when the food arrived. Other physical needs that will arise in time are arranging play dates for any children impacted to give them a brief respite from the grief, picking up family members from the airport, and doing the yard work. In all these situations, you are meeting a need that the person impacted by the suddenness of grief does not have the mental bandwidth to think about.

SPEAK CAREFULLY

One last word to those of you walking alongside someone experiencing the suddenness of grief, be careful with the words you say. The best thing you can say is, "I'm sorry." Let silence communicate your love. Too often our words add more pain to the grieving heart. "Like one who takes away a garment on a cold day, or like vinegar poured on a wound, is one who sings songs to a heavy heart" (Proverbs 25:20). Cheerfulness around those who are grieving is like ripping away someone's coat on a cold day or pouring acid on a wound. To help, here are seven statements that many think will help, but rarely do in the initial stages of loss:

Seven statements NEVER to say:

- *"You'll be ok"*
- *"At least…"*
- *"It's for the best…"*
- *"I know how you feel"*
- *"Keep a stiff upper lip"*
- *"You should"/ "You shouldn't" (don't give advice)*
- *"God doesn't give us more than we can handle"*

A good rule to follow is to let those who've lost be the pace setter of talking: don't talk more than they do. To help you with this, remember to WAIT—ask "**W**hy **A**m **I** **T**alking?"

The suddenness of grief demands our attention. It brutally interrupts our "regularly scheduled programming" for tragedy and chaos. In these first moments of grieving, take heart—the journey has just begun, but you are not alone. In the next chapter, we will discover who is with you as you live in the grief.

CHAPTER 3
THE RANDOMNESS OF GRIEF

THE CRY OF WHY?

This is not fair. My mind could not comprehend the words I just heard. "I think Adam died" was what my daughter-in-law said but I honestly thought she meant Adam was just in distress and there was still hope. When her sister called to confirm Adam's passing, my world began to spin. My mind cried out to God, "What just happened?"

I found myself trying to understand what happened, but I ended up giving God a list of reasons why this should not have happened at all. Adam was a youth pastor, a young married man with a child about to be born. I was a lifelong pastor. I had lived rightly as best I could. Why would this happen to us? This did not make sense.

Debbie's Journey

In the moments of hearing that my son was in some type of distress I knew in my gut that what I would hear next would be even worse. I did my best in that short moment of scrambling to get my things together and get in the car to drive with my husband and teenage son to where Adam was, thinking "I better hear good news!" Then Dave's phone rang, and he didn't even say a word and I knew just watching his face "He's GONE?" What? How?

I hit the ground bending over crying out in the loudest cries of pain I have ever felt. My heart felt as if it leaped out of my body and I couldn't breathe, I cried out to Jesus. The next thing I remember is asking Jesus to be with Adam and to help me.

When Dave could finally get me off the ground, we realized we needed help, we needed to leave immediately to get out to be with Adam's wife. We called our friends Shelli and Jake—I knew they would come, and they were at our place within five minutes to drive us the 60 miles to their apartment. That drive out to Adam was horrendous as my brain couldn't comprehend that this happened. All I knew is that Adam was gone, and I was worried about his wife and their baby. I had to call our daughter Aimee, and she was already on her way to Adam's apartment. So were my close cousins who abandoned a vacation to come hold us.

In my head I knew we would be the last to arrive being the furthest away, though the chaos we encountered was still not what I had ever hoped or expected it to be. That is all I can say without too much detail of when we arrived—because all in all it was the biggest nightmare for me, and I was in such disarray that I could barely focus on any conversation. My brain was so clouded and all I wanted to hear was that my son didn't suffer. A medic could only tell us that it seemed as if it was instantaneous due to no trauma being found, but I could never get an answer as to why this happened?

On the "outside," Adam appeared to be a healthy, energetic, active young man with his whole life ahead of him. I could not see the ticking time-bomb inside him, that weak blood vessel in his brain that was about to burst and instantly take his life. The randomness of grief did not allow me to prepare for what was to happen next.

The only aspect of grief that is worse than the suddenness of grief is its randomness. Suffering, loss, and grief do not follow a prescribed formula. While some illnesses or dire consequences have a logical connection to a past behavior, the randomness of grief hits without warning. The unannounced crashes through the "front door" of our lives like a car swerving off a road and into an innocent home. The victims are enjoying life as it should be for them until they are forced to deal with tragedy and mayhem with no preparation. The randomness of grief is the second emotional hit after the suddenness of grief, and causes us to cry, "Why?"

If we are honest about our practical system of beliefs, each of holds to a version of Karma. We expect good things to happen to good people and bad things happen to bad people. This is how life usually operates in general terms. However, the randomness of grief implies that at times, more often than we care to admit, bad things do happen to good people. This challenges our faith system, and, for the Christian, we question the sovereignty of God. "How could a loving God allow this?"

JOB'S STORY

Which brings us to the story of Job… The story of Job begins in Heaven, with God pointing out the faith of Job. Satan claimed Job only obeyed God because God had blessed Job with wealth and health, so God allowed Satan to inflict suffering upon Job to test Job's reason for faith. Job had his large stock of animals stolen, and all his farmhands were killed. His house was destroyed, killing his children … ALL in the same day.

Yet in the midst of suffering Job still praised God: "And he said, 'Naked I came from my mother's womb, and naked shall I return. The LORD gave, and the LORD has taken away; blessed be the name of the LORD.' In all this Job did not sin or charge God with wrong" (Job 1:21–22). Later, Job contracted a terrible case of boils from head to foot. And as he sat in misery scraping his running sores with broken pieces of pottery, the only comfort and advice he got from his wife was, "Curse God and die" (Job 2:9). "But [Job] said to her, "You speak as one of the foolish women would speak. Shall we receive good from God, and shall we not receive [trouble]?" In all this Job did not sin with his lips" (Job 2:10, ESV).

Finally, Job broke and instead of blaming God, Job cursed the day he was born (Job 3:1–3) and asked a deep question, "Why is light given to a man whose way is hidden, whom God has hedged in? For my sighing comes instead of my bread, and my groanings are poured out like water. For the thing that I fear comes upon me, and what I dread befalls me" (Job 3:23–25, ESV). Essentially asking, "Why is life given to those with no future, to those who God has purposed to live in distress?"

Job could not understand why God would allow such suffering. "Only grant me two things, then I will not hide myself from your face: withdraw your hand far from me, and let not dread of you terrify me. Then call, and I will answer; or let me speak, and you reply to me" (Job 13:20–22, ESV). Job in his suffering begged for two things: relief from his suffering, and God's presence so he could get answers to a reason for his suffering. Job wanted to know "why?" We are the same. We can accept the hardship if we have a reason that explains it cause. This would allow us to predict it, anticipate it, and perhaps even prepare ourselves emotionally and spiritually for the suffering. To be caught off guard—that we could be surprised by suffering that seems random—terrifies us!

The main portion of the book of Job is a series of discussions in the form of poems between Job and his friends. His friends still held onto the idea of retribution—that God is just, and the world is fair, therefore Job must have done something very wrong. They even accused him of hypothetical sins they assumed he'd done, but each time Job defended himself. Job was on this emotional roller coaster: at one point trusting in God and the next moment doubting God's goodness. Finally, Job couldn't handle the randomness of his suffering any longer and demanded to meet with God.

This demand from Job brings us to chapter 38. Curiously, God had not been seen since chapter 2. God did not have a direct role during Job's crisis even though Job had been desperate for an explanation from God. However, after the series of discussions with Job's friends concluded, God spoke, "Then the Lord spoke to Job out of the storm" (Job 38:1, NIV).

Job's life felt like an emotional and spiritual storm, yet God used a physical storm as the backdrop for His divine presence. This nature scene reminds us that the power of God cannot be controlled by human intentions just like the powerful wind of a tornado in uncontainable. This chaotic scene humbles Job. While the randomness of grief had given Job a "case" against the power and sovereignty of

God, the power of the storm reveals how hollow and superficial those arguments were. God continued to address Job:

> *Who is this that obscures my plans with words without knowledge? Brace yourself like a man; I will question you, and you shall answer me. "Where were you when I laid the earth's foundation? Tell me, if you understand. Who marked off its dimensions? Surely you know! Who stretched a measuring line across it? On what were its footings set, or who laid its cornerstone—while the morning stars sang together and all the angels shouted for joy?"* (Job 38:2–7, NIV).

God told Job to prepare for His perspective. God was putting Job on notice that Job's thinking and rationale was wrong. The randomness of grief had led Job to ask God, "Why?" and to demand answers to the deep question of grief. However, God pointed out that Job was asking to know God's plan without having true knowledge about the nature of life. Life has an intelligent design that gives it a sense of order, but that does not equate to a fairness of experiences. We demand life be fair; we seek to implement laws and policies that create a sense of fairness for all people. However, a difficult reality to accept is that life is never fair. God's plan was not to give everyone equal opportunities in life but to restore all people to Himself through the unique situations He allows each to be placed in. God gives each person these opportunities as He "marked out their appointed times in history and the boundaries of their lands. God did this so that they would seek him and perhaps reach out for him and find him" (Acts 17:26–27, NIV). Notice this implies each person's opportunities would be different from another person as their appointed times and places were different, but this would not prevent someone from seeking God.

Life is not fair as not everyone has the same opportunities: some would have more, some less opportunities in life. Yet, life does not have to be fair for people to come to God. What appears random to us—the course of our life's events—is not random to God. God marked out times, ordained boundaries; God has a plan for your life and that allows for the suddenness and randomness of grief. God was preparing Job to understand his position in life and that the randomness of grief is not something Job could understand.

As you read the complete interaction between God and Job, you will notice God does not tell Job about the heavenly challenges from Satan. This is the most frustrating part of Job's story to me. There was a reason Job went through the suffering. It was not random but an intentional test of his faith. Yet, God never revealed this to Job. But does knowing the cause of the suffering make the situation any better? I don't think so; it's like you have an itch, but once you scratch it, you begin to feel the itch in many more places. I think to know the suffering was the result of Satan's inquiry would not diminish the randomness of grief, as it would just create more questions. Therefore, God does not explain why the suffering happened but instead God took Job on a virtual tour of the universe to give Job a broader perspective.

The first question God asked Job was a rhetorical question: "where were you?" (38:4). Where were you when I created the world, the oceans, and the sun? God pointed out the great details in the universe, things we see every day but don't understand.

> *"Have you ever given orders to the morning, or shown the dawn its place, that it might take the earth by the edges and shake the wicked out of it?"* (Job 38:12–13, NIV).

"Who cuts a channel for the torrents of rain, and a path for the thunderstorm, to water a land where no one lives, an uninhabited desert, to satisfy a desolate wasteland and make it sprout with grass?" (Job 38:25–27, NIV).

God asked Job if he even understood the complexities of the world. God asked Job if he could control nature's forces?

"Do you know the laws of the heavens? Can you set up God's dominion over the earth?" (Job 38:33, NIV).

From Job's point of view—it looked like God was not just, but God's perspective is so much bigger. God is interacting with the dynamics of the universe in ways we can't understand. This is the unknowable way of God considering all the complexities of the universe when He makes decisions.

Job didn't have an answer for God—but humbly learned to accept his life as it was.

Then Job answered the LORD: "I am unworthy—how can I reply to you? I put my hand over my mouth. I spoke once, but I have no answer—twice, but I will say no more" (Job 40:3–5, NIV).

The Hebrew word Job used here means, "of no weight."[3] Job, in the presence of the majesty of God, confessed insignificance. Job never learned why he suffered, but he was able to live in peace and in fear of the Lord. David Guzik points out, "The different tone was not

[3] Strong's Lexicon, "H7043 – qālal," https://www.blueletterbible.org/lexicon/h7043/kjv/wlc/0-1/.

because Job's circumstances had substantially changed. He was still in misery and had lost virtually everything. The tone changed because while he once felt that God had forsaken him, now he felt and knew that God was with Him."[4] Job had experienced the promised presence of God in difficult times, and Job responded to all that God had shown him:

> *I know that you can do all things, and that no purpose of yours can be thwarted. "Who is this that hides counsel without knowledge?" Therefore I have uttered what I did not understand, things too wonderful for me, which I did not know... I had heard of you by the hearing of the ear, but now my eye sees you* (Job 42:2–3, 5, ESV).

Job' focus was no longer on receiving an answer to his suffering question, but his focus was on God, whom he trusted to know what He was doing. The power of Job's story is that God does not answer the question of "Why Suffering?" but rather refocuses upon the "Who?" Who is worthy to be trusted? *Who is with you* in the suffering. Only God is! When Job experienced the fullness of God, he had no more questions, he humbly realized that the randomness of grief does not eliminate God but rather shines the spotlight on the truth that God transcends our circumstances.[5] Job confessed that he had a basic understanding about God, which left him asking questions for God to justify himself; but now he had come to know God, and that was all he needed (Job 42:5). Job's final words to God were

---

[4] David Guzik, "Study Guide for Job 40," https://www.blueletterbible.org/comm/guzik_david/study-guide/job/job-40.cfm.

[5] Jerry L. Sittser, *A Grace Disguised Revised and Expanded: How the Soul Grows Through Loss* (Zondervan publishing, 2021) 101.

his repentance and humble surrender to God (Job 42:6). This was the beginning of Job's restoration in life after grief.

THE RANDOMNESS OF GRIEF'S IMPACT ON US

I was going to label this section "Understanding the Randomness of Grief," but then I realized that is the exact issue with "randomness": it is unexplainable, there is no understanding it. Therefore, the impact of the randomness of grief upon us is more complex. Unlike the suddenness of grief, which takes its toil upon our physical, mental, and emotional systems through stress, the randomness of grief impacts our faith support system. The randomness of loss and suffering makes it difficult to accept the situation as part of God's will, but as we saw with the purpose of the story Job in the Bible, the randomness of grief and suffering doesn't have to diminish our faith in God.

James the apostle looked back on the life of Job as an example to follow. "Behold, we consider those blessed who remained steadfast. You have heard of the steadfastness of Job, and you have seen the purpose of the Lord, how the Lord is compassionate and merciful" (James 5:11, ESV). This word steadfastness can also be translated "patience"; however, this word does not describe a passive waiting but an active endurance. In the context of the Greek text, it is the quality that helps you finish a marathon. The root word in Greek means *to remain under*.[6] It has the picture of someone under a heavy load and choosing to stay there instead of trying to escape.

---

[6] Strong's Lexicon, "G5281 – *hypomonē*," https://www.blueletterbible.org/lexicon/g5281/kjv/tr/0-1/.

It is not easy to remain in the grief. We want to quickly escape it, but that will stifle our healing process and dishonor the one we love. By choosing to be steadfast, we learn more about ourselves and who God is. As James said, it was through remaining steadfast that Job saw a greater depth to the work of God in the world and understood the full character of God. Job learned the mystery that in the randomness of grief, he could experience God's compassion and mercy. What a combination to feel at your darkest moment. I cried out for God's mercy. I could often barely breathe out, "God give us mercy." In the mysterious work of God, I can look back now, a couple years removed from Adam's passing and see the compassionate and merciful hand of God protecting us from further pain. I cannot describe the events because I believe in God's mercy, He shielded us so we could remain steadfast in the little strength we had in ourselves as He was compassionately carrying us along. One of the greatest choices you can make is to allow yourself to be cared for and carried by God.

I learned that I have a choice of how I will respond to the grief. It did not feel this way at first because grief had robbed me of my normal operating system: how I think and feel in normal situations. We thrive in an ordered world. Even those whose life resembles "chaos embodied" still have a standard routine they follow. You most likely sleep in the same bed every night, on the same side of the bed and in the same position (I'm a side sleeper myself). If you or I were to spend the night in a different bed, we probably would not get as good a night's worth of sleep because it is an unfamiliar bed, but I bet you still slept on the same side of the bed as you normally do and in the same position (as best as possible). Order. Structure. The familiar. All these characteristics help us move through our day with as little stress as possible. We don't have to overthink these decisions because we know what we enjoy and what works for us. The randomness of grief severs the familiar. Suddenly it takes great mental energy to make a simple decision like what should I eat when I eventually do get hungry. The known has become the unknown and that scares us. The ability to choose how we will respond in the grief is challenged by a flood of emotions, fears, and hormones stimulating our brain and body's "fight or flight" mode. But as difficult as it may be to make, we still have a choice.

I live by the beach and have found great comfort by staring at the waves pounding the shoreline. I have learned I cannot stop the waves, but I can learn how to surf. That is my choice. I can surf the wave; I can choose to jump the wave; I often choose to turn my back to the wave and let it crash over me. The waves will still come but I will always have choices that I can make. While the randomness of grief may impact me emotionally and spiritually, I can choose how I respond. Job chose to remain steadfast in his faith in God. Job's endurance of suffering produced an integrity in his relationship with God. He would be able to say to Satan, if he knew the whole story, "I don't follow God just because He gives me good things … I follow Him because He is God." What will you be able to say because of how you choose to respond to the randomness of grief?

FOR THOSE LIVING IN THE RANDOMNESS OF GRIEF

ALLOW YOURSELF TO GRIEVE HONESTLY

Do not feel like you need to move on quickly to accepting the loss. For us to "grieve with hope," we first must grieve and not just hope. However, too often Christians feel they are slighting God by feeling the pain, questioning God's judgment, or not desiring to praise God for blessings. Before Debbie and I were finally able to return to worship God with our church family (we had been absent for ten weeks), I wrote the church a letter…

DEAR CORNERSTONE FAMILY,

The Cornerstone Family is truly a family of families! Debbie, Mfundo, and I have felt extremely loved and cared for by you all over the past few months. Thank you to all of you for your prayers, cards, flowers, meals, gifts, and words of compassion. We realize many of you are grieving alongside us, shedding tears for our family and for our church.

We still deal daily with the shock of our son Adam's passing. We know God is still good and in control, and we look forward to seeing all that God will be doing through this difficult journey through a dark valley.

Therefore, as we re-engage with you at church, please know we want to be there, even if we may seem distant at moments. We are worshipping with you, even if we are not singing. We love you, even if we are not able to hug you at this time.

I (Dave) look forward to leading and teaching you what God has been teaching me during this season, even if it may be delayed for now. To this end—when you see us, instead of asking "how are you?"—just tell us, "I'm glad to see you" or "I'm praying for you." We are not able to answer that question but will still welcome your intentions to show your concern and love.

The intent of this letter was to inform our church of how to best understand and love us. Notice the permission we were giving ourselves: we were going to attend a worship service but not sing, be with people but not give hugs. I was the teaching pastor of the church, but I needed to be honest about my grief and not try to mask it with false joy. We were going to take the time we needed to grieve, even grieve in public. You need to give yourself permission to do the same; take the time you need to experience the fullness of grief so you can heal.

Debbie's Journey

I only knew how to grieve by doing what I normally did before our loss. I continued to read Scripture and began to focus on learning how to lament in my mourning. I also found great comfort in reading books and learning from others who knew of or experienced similar loss. I especially felt that I needed some counsel in the way I was grieving, which was very different from others in my family. My grief kept coming at me like rough ocean waves, giving me few moments of relief in these turbulent times. I found my ultimate comfort came from the time I was able to have with my Savior in solitude. I had this time before our loss, and I know that my time with Him is where I feel heard and known.

PRAY THE PSALMS OF LAMENT

God's inspired truth includes worship poems, i.e. psalms, that are difficult to understand. These worship psalms were written by men who were in danger or in pain. We call these Psalms of Lament. They are God's way of helping us work through the question of suffering and hardship. They are meant to be sung in public worship at the temple and prayed in private. These prayers of lament are important because the Bible never answers why God allows suffering, which causes us to question God's justice, even God's character. The structure of a psalm of lament is very specific and guides a worshiper through confessing both the pain of life as well as trust in God. There are five parts to a psalm of lament: a summary of the problem, an explanation of life's painful or overwhelming circumstances, the request for change or relief, a confession of trust in God to provide that deliverance, and finally a renewed vow of praise. The confession of trust in God keeps this prayer from becoming a pity party and instead refocuses the worshiper upon God, enabling the person to continue in faithfulness to God.

Psalm 13 is a powerful psalm of Lament that I prayed over and over in the most intense season of grief.

How long, LORD? Will you forget me forever?
How long will you hide your face from me?
How long must I wrestle with my thoughts
and day after day have sorrow in my heart?
How long will my enemy triumph over me?

Look on me and answer, LORD my God.
Give light to my eyes, or I will sleep in death,
and my enemy will say, "I have overcome him,"
and my foes will rejoice when I fall.

But I trust in your unfailing love;
my heart rejoices in your salvation.
I will sing the LORD's praise,
for he has been good to me

(Psalm 13:1–6, NIV).

King David wrote this psalm in a time of despair and discouragement. I identified with this psalm of lament because I was wrestling with the randomness of grief and the deep sorrow in my heart. I wondered how long I had to stumble around in the darkness and wanted God to give me relief (the request of verse 3). In my prayer time, I kept repeating the breath prayer "I trust in your unfailing love," the confession of trust in this psalm of lament (verse 5). I could not rejoice yet, but I was trying to daily look for the goodness of God. This was my renewed vow of praise (verse 6): God is still good, and I will bend my will to acknowledge that, even if in my pain it was difficult to admit. In my study of the Psalms of Lament, I found that one-third of all the psalms in the Bible are laments. This tells us God is okay with us pouring out our pain to Him as He seeks to comfort us. Praying the Psalms of Laments does not make life instantly easier or better but this practice does place our hearts in a position of trust in God, which is the first and best position to be in when dealing with the randomness of grief.

FOR THOSE WALKING ALONGSIDE THOSE WHO ARE GRIEVING

When you see someone grieving, you will experience a natural reaction to provide comfort. However, in this attempt to encourage the brokenhearted, don't try to stop them from expressing their pain or rush them to get "over" it. Don't try to "fix them." It's uncomfortable to be with someone in deep grief but you need to sit in the pain with them. Remember, Job's friends gave amazing comfort as they sat with him in silence for those first seven days. It was only when they opened their mouths and tried to reason with Job, seeking to explain away the pain, that they inflicted more pain upon Job. In fact, Job said to his friends after their first round of speeches, "I have heard many things like these; you are miserable comforters, all of you!" (Job 16:1–2, NIV).

We should all take seriously God's rebuke of Job's friends at the end of the book of Job. As God restored Job, He said to Eliphaz, "I am angry with you and your two friends, because you have not spoken the truth about me, as my servant Job has," (Job 42:7, NIV) and calls their words of comfort to Job "folly" (verse 8). God only forgave the friends when Job prayed for them. What a rebuke! The good intentions of the friends to rush Job out of grief and into recovery was foolishness in the sight of God and worthy of punishment. May we not be as foolish before the Lord and simply sit with those we love who are grieving.

Debbie's Journey

Dave and I are now being asked by others how they should help their loved ones in their own grief and loss. This is something I take very seriously because we have experienced both sides of it the good and bad. Do not ever feel something needs to be said other than "sorry for your loss," "thinking & praying for you," or "I love you." These are the best statements and will always be accepted and heard. People in grief do not want to listen to your experience. I once got asked how I was doing by someone who had experienced loss, and I answered by saying, "I am in very deep pain." I was crying as I answered them, but they could not handle it. They couldn't be around me in my grief and pain, so they turned and left without saying a word, not knowing that they had made my grief worse. Please handle with care those around you who are grieving.

Please listen to two final warnings: don't make promises you can't keep (i.e. if you need anything—just ask…). While you truly want to do what will be needed, the reality is your life will most likely return to normal in a few weeks, when the real needs start appearing, and you will not have the time to meet the requests of the grieving person. Many friendships have ended as those in grief quickly learn who will keep their promise and can be relied upon for help and who only gave them pity.

Lastly, don't try to explain God if the grieving person is angry with God—God will reveal Himself to the grieving heart in due time. This was the mistake of Job's friends; they were trying to find a spiritual reason for the suffering and loss Job had experienced. Instead of simply sitting with Job, quietly praying for Job, they tried to explain the way of God in our lives in the limited ways they understood. Please do not give into that same temptation. Allow God to be the one who brings the ultimate comfort. Be present. Be available. Be praying. Be quiet.

The randomness of grief is a challenge that will never be understood but it does not need to be. While we may never be able to understand the *why* of the loss, we can be assured of *Who* is walking with us in our journey in the shadow of grief. God is present with us. This will be the focus of the next chapter.

CHAPTER 4

THE QUESTION OF GRIEF

As the reality of Adam's death settled upon me, I was shaken by the question of, "Where was God in that moment?" I wondered why God did not intervene in a miraculous way as He did in the all the biblical stories that I learned. I questioned why Adam was not given a second chance at life like Lazarus was given and so many others that have been medically saved. In the moment of that dreadful phone call, I remember crying out to God for help and taking comfort in knowing Adam was in the presence of Jesus in that instant. The following weeks I studied the theology of Heaven with vigor as I realized I had a cartoonish view of the afterlife. However, as much comfort as I took in the reality of Heaven, I could not shake the feeling that God had somehow failed my family. How could I doubt His faithfulness? God had provided and protected my family many times in the past;

yet at this moment, I doubted. I wrestled with the tension of believing but needing someone to help me with my unbelief. That living in the tension of belief and doubt morphed into me asking, "Where is God in this moment?"

LIVING WITH GOD IN THIS MOMENT

Some of you may feel uneasy with my journey of faith, with a greater emphasis on my doubts than assurances; but without acknowledging your doubts and struggles you will never arrive at a moment of surrender. This is what faith is: surrendering control to God because you believe He is enough. Faith is recognizing God is faithful but still being disappointed in His answer to my request. The faith of the brokenhearted keeps trusting God even though life is less than our desired outcomes. It does not take scientific proof to have this level of faith. It takes enough evidence to believe beyond a reasonable doubt. I live with reasonable doubt, much like the father of the demonic-possessed child who ask Jesus to help him if He [Jesus] could. "'If you can'?" said Jesus. "Everything is possible for one who believes." Immediately the boy's father exclaimed, 'I do believe; help me overcome my unbelief!'" (Mark 9:23–24, NIV). I am so grateful the Holy Spirit prompted Mark to include this story, as it is the affirmation I needed to know that living in the tension of belief and doubt was acceptable to God, as Jesus immediately healed the child after this confession from the father (verse 25).

God knows I am on a journey of faith; and He is okay with my inability to sing worship songs whose lines conflict with my doubt. I believe God delights in my authentic declaration of His goodness despite feeling His silence in songs like "Altogether Good" by the band Citizens. When Adam passed—I turned first to the Psalms of Lament to cry out to God, but eventually I found Psalm 116 and it became my "Life Raft." I read it every day for a month. I read it slowly and meditated on just a verse or two at a time. However, what I thought was a psalm of lament was actually a psalm of praise—looking at my past need and how God responded, looking at God's character and how I will live each day. Within the midst of suffering, God is present and desires for us to turn to Him and affirm what we know to be true of Him alone. If you are on a journey with grief, you may not be ready to consider these truths now, but Psalm 116 gives us insight on how to live with God in this moment of grief and my hope is this will lead you from times of darkness to sustaining peace.

Let us first consider the literary context of Psalm 116. Psalms 113–118 were written as praises that were sung in connection with the Passover meal and other Jewish holidays and reflect upon God's redemption of His people, particularly from their bondage in Egypt. These were sung all together as an extended expression of praise and thanks to God for the many kindnesses bestowed upon Israel. This means that when Jesus was with His disciples on the night of His betrayal and arrest, which we commonly refer to as the Last Supper, he sang Psalm 116. ("When they had sung a hymn, they went out to the Mount of Olives" Matthew 26:30, NIV.) Jesus sang Psalm 116 as He knew He was going to the cross! Think about that, Jesus, facing death, sang this psalm of praise.

The psalmist began his song (Psalm 116:1–2) with a confession of grateful love; but for many of us, God's attentiveness to our problems and needs is a great gift that we take for granted. Think about it—the Almighty God in the universe, with all the complexities of the world and all its people, still knows your voice, hears your cries for help, and turns to you. In the moment of loss, it is easy to feel like God has forgotten you, therefore this psalm begins with a reminder of the hard truth that God is still present in our times of grieving.

Yet the psalmist is using this song to reflect on an intense season of sorrow as verse 3 declares, “The cords of death entangled me, the anguish of the grave came over me; I was overcome by distress and sorrow” (NIV). The Hebrew word for *cords* literally is a rope, or better a noose, therefore this word is often translated as sorrows, pain, destruction, or ruin in figurative terms.[7] In other words, the events of the psalmist’s life were so severe it felt like a rope was wrapped around his neck and squeezing off his life. This description is parallel to the distress and anguish of the “grave”; this is the Hebrew word for Hell, *Sheol*, the Old Testament designation for the abode of the dead.[8] The resulting feeling was being overcome with trouble and sorrow to the point of longing for death itself to be the only source of relief. This is a very dark place to be emotionally and spiritually, yet it where we often find ourselves when dealing with tragic loss and feeling God is absent in the moment.

This is how I have felt at times since Adam’s death. I have struggled with the reality God has allowed my family to endure but it is good to admit the struggle because the psalmist claimed the same thing here in God’s inspired Word. Being in this desperate state, the psalmist did what many of us do in crisis—he cries out to God. Notice how simple and to the point this prayer is “Lord, save me” (verse 4). Peter prayed the same prayer when he was walking on water to Jesus, but looked away to the storm, and began to sink. He also cried out “Lord, save me” and Jesus reached out and “caught him” (Matthew 14:30–31, NIV). I love that wording, Jesus “caught” him. While the word *caught* means “to lay hold of” in the original Greek language, it

---

[7] Strong’s Lexicon, “H2256 – *ḥēḇel*,” https://www.blueletterbible.org/lexicon/h2256/kjv/wlc/0-1/.

[8] Strong’s Lexicon, “H7585 – *šᵊʾôl*,” https://www.blueletterbible.org/lexicon/h7585/kjv/wlc/0-1/.

can also be used metaphorically to imply "to rescue one from peril, to help."[9] Whether or not we are able to recognize God reaching out His hand to catch us, God is present. Regardless of our feelings, God is rescuing us and helping us. Therefore, as you are able, the key to living with God in the moment of grief is to remember and meditate on God's character.

God has a trustworthy character. The wonder of Psalm 116 is that while the psalmist was remembering his intense sorrow, he was also remembering God's rescuing action. Verses 5–9 are full of statements of God's character and action that are praiseworthy. The psalmist began to reflect on God's deliverance by first recognizing God's character:

> *God is gracious—gives us what we don't deserve.*
>
> *God is righteous—does what is consistently right and good.*
>
> *God is full of compassion—spares us the punishment and destruction we truly deserve.*

Paul echoed this reality of God by declaring, "But God, being rich in mercy, because of the great love with which he loved us, even when we were dead in our trespasses, made us alive together with Christ—by grace you have been saved" (Ephesians 2:4–5, ESV). The result of God's action and goodness is I can be at rest (Psalm116:7). The Hebrew grammar of the word *rest* is in the plural, indicating

---

[9] Strong's Lexicon, "G1949 – *epilambanomai,*" https://www.blueletterbible.org/lexicon/g1949/kjv/tr/0-1/.

complete rest, at all times, and under all circumstances.[10] This is the opposite of how the psalmist felt in verse 3, when he was overcome with anguish and sorrow. This is what those who are grieving want: rest from the trouble, the sorrow, and the burden of what happened. This is possible to experience when we recognize God's goodness is still present in our lives. I think the end of verse 7 is the psalmist talking to himself, making himself acknowledge God is still good. I am learning this as well, to take stock of God's presence and goodness in my life amid tragedy and grief. Debbie and I try to practice this as we take our daily walk, thanking God for time with our family. This is a spiritual exercise of Faith. It doesn't just happen, rather it happens through being intentional with your time with God—meditating on God's Word and God's actions.

Debbie's Journey

The day Adam passed away, as others joined us and brought our family food for nourishment and Adam's pastor was there for support and Adam's coworkers as well, I will never forget the amazing time with the Lord we had together. We had a beautiful time of prayer and crying out to God in the heavens for Him to hear! The beautiful prayers being lifted to Jesus about how grateful we were for Adam and the gift he was to so many. This kind of crying out to God continued for me until I felt numb.

---

[10] Strong's Lexicon, "H4496 – mᵊ*nûḥâ,*" https://www.blueletterbible.org/lexicon/h4496/kjv/wlc/0-1/.

The power of Psalm 116 is the praise of God matches the greatness of God's deliverance. The psalmist gives us a statement of confidence, "that I may walk before the LORD in the land of the living" (verse 9, NIV), as the full result of God's deliverance, both now and forever in Heaven. Walking before the LORD means walking in the waiting. Waiting for God is waiting in faith-filled expectation of what God alone can do. This is how we live with God now: waiting in expectation. In the New Testament we have similar phrases: "walk by faith," "walk in the light"; each of these statements is full of demanding obedience but also of confident assurance of God's presence and promises. Waiting therefore is trusting in God (Psalm 116:10) not in our own strength and wisdom.

A psalm of praise concludes with a renewed vow of obedience, which had the psalmist confessing his salvation in God alone and his obedience to God (Psalm 116:12–14). The psalmist then paused in verse 15 to consider the evidence we belong to the Lord, that the Lord is pleased with our lives, so He considers our death precious. When I first read these words after Adam's passing, I did not know what to do with them. But then I remembered my thoughts of Adam standing before Jesus on the day he entered Heaven, hearing the words from his Master "... '*Well done, good and faithful servant!* You have been faithful with a few things; I will put you in charge of many things. Come and share your master's happiness!'" (Matthew 25:21, NIV, emphasis mine). It brings tears to my eyes when I consider God's pleasure in Adam. A pleasure that was able to be fully experienced for the first time when Adam heard "Well done"! To commemorate that reality, I had tattooed on my arm the line from the song "Endless Praise" by Charity Gayle, "Standing with those who have heard well done." What a thought, though death is a curse and an enemy, it is still precious because it removes the remaining barriers between God and His saints and is the doorway to an eternity of perfect fellowship.

Because death couldn't hold Jesus, death can't hold Adam. Death won't hold me. This is what we wait for to be alive with God and our loved ones forever, and that is our destiny!

WALKING WITH OTHERS IN THEIR DOUBTS OF GOD

You have noticed I have discussed many Scriptures in this chapter as a model of how to walk alongside someone in grief: allow God to do the talking. Within Psalm 119, a powerful psalm describing the Word of God, we read a verse that proclaims what we all need from God and His Word, "My soul is weary with sorrow; strengthen me according to your word" (verse 28, NIV). The key is to know when to share Scripture and when to allow someone to find its comforting truth on their own. When in doubt, wait a little longer to share a key psalm or promise from God's Word. Some of the most encouraging reminders of God's truth came a month or longer after Adam's passing. This was the season that the Scriptures we initially held onto began to become routine, when other family and friends had to return to their "regularly scheduled" lives leaving us to fend off grief in greater isolation. It is at that moment that God would pierce the darkness through a well-timed note of prayer and Scripture. It was Heaven-sent "rain" nourishing our dry souls. Thank God for wise Christ-followers who were sensitive to our need and allowed God to speak to us through them.

I understand waiting is so hard to do. I don't wait well. I tend to rush the process. However, when walking alongside someone in grief, the process is important. The butterfly must struggle to emerge from its cocoon, to develop the strength to fly and live. Even the well-intentioned effort to free the butterfly prematurely, removing the struggle, is an act of condemning that butterfly to death as it will never fly and will be an easy target of prey. The same is true for someone going through grief; they alone must do the struggle of emerging from this long season of grief. If we rush the process, we subject them to even greater pain. Therefore, my encouragement to you is to be patient and take what the grieving person can give you. Patience is our only option because we are not in control. Patience is a tool God uses to mature our faith as we must humbly admit and accept that we are not in control. We are not sovereign as God is. God is working both in the grieving heart and in your life as you wait. Waiting has a purpose. Waiting expands our capacity to grieve with hope as we learn to live in the grace of God. Therefore, do not rush someone through their grief. As painful and uncomfortable as it is to watch them struggle, be present, be silent, and wait.

Debbie's Journey

My therapist Karen has taught me to pause in moments when I feel the need to react. In my grief there have been many of these moments. I have had many conversations with the Lord about this. It usually sounds like this...Lord I want to slap that person; Lord I feel like I should say this or that! These are the times I have with God, and He shows me how patient He is with me and how grace giving He is with me that I then turn to say nothing to someone, or I later pray for them. These moments that I choose to pause instead of reacting have been lessons to chat with others about how God is using my grief to reflect who He is in my life.

Lastly, do not feel as if it your responsibility to defend God. The wounded heart may say things that sound offensive or a mischaracterization of God's character. If God can take the emotional outbursts of the psalmists and Elijah (1 Kings 19), then God can endure the anger shouts from the grieving person. The deep pain causes doubts in God's goodness; this new doubt in a previously undoubted God creates a surge at anger: anger at the situation and at God for allowing it, and even anger at themselves for having these doubts. The unknowable is too much for our finite minds and limited faith to reckon with so do not give into the temptation to try and explain it by defending a God who can defend himself. Remember you did not have any input into creating the crisis and so you are not responsible to solve the problem. Allow space for God to work, to bring justice in His timing and His way.

About a year after Adam passed away, my wife and I felt we needed a change of scenery; the old house was too full of old memories. We bought a new house and before we moved in, we undertook a large remodeling project that touched almost everything about the inside of this new purchase. We had a tight timeframe to finish the remodeling before we had to be out of our former house. For the first month I would go visit the house to check on the progress of the workers, and it seemed to be stuck in continual demolition mode. I would walk in the front door onto broken tiles, to cabinets that were removed, bathrooms that were unusable. Walking around I was discouraged at the slow pace, but my wife and I had to remind ourselves it would not always be in this state, and we would say to each other, "Can't wait until we start replacing and rebuilding." That is all of us: Broken Vessels. We are those pieces, broken and scattered, that God in mercy has gathered, raising up the broken to life! As you walk alongside someone in the shadow of grief, allow God's mercy to do His resurrection work; your grieving loved one will thank you for the unhurried time to heal.

SECTION 2
RESPONDING TO GRIEF

We hope this next section of the book is especially helpful to those of you who are able to process the loss you experienced; perhaps it would be best to think of these chapters as the first, second, and third responses to sudden loss and grief, and not to necessarily try to activate all these responses at the same time. However, before we seek to discuss our responses to grief, it will be helpful to solidify our faith foundation by seeking to form a theology of grief by looking into God's perspective on grief and its impact on our faith.

CHAPTER 5

GOD'S PERSPECTIVE OF GRIEF

Grief causes us to question God, as if God had failed us. An informed theology of grief requires us to pursue these questions with an authentic and honest consideration of God's action, or lack thereof. I was not the first to question if God had failed me in the moment. The psalmist and worship leader Asaph wrote a scathing question of God in Psalm 77.

Will the Lord reject forever?
Will he never show his favor again?
Has his unfailing love vanished forever?
Has his promise failed for all time?
(Psalm 77:7–8, NIV).

The psalmist began this worship poem similar to many Psalms of Lament, with a crying out to God (verse 1). His grief was so great, he refused to be comforted (verse 2). Who would refuse comfort? The better question is "why" would Asaph not receive comfort? It was because he was not receiving comfort from the One who mattered most to him: God. Read his confession in verse 3, "*I remembered you, God, and I groaned*; I meditated, and my spirit grew faint" (NIV, emphasis added). The problem was not Asaph failing to call out to God in his crisis, it was that when he groaned for God, he did not receive the comfort from God that he begged for. The master musician Asaph included the musical notation *Selah* at the end of verse 3 to allow time for the singers, the musicians and all who were listening and reading to pause in order to reflect more deeply on this reality. To take a breath and ponder the depth of his emotional and spiritual pain, Asaph cried out to God. He remembered God, and he grew tired of waiting for God to respond. It is as if Asaph was crying out "God, I know you are there … where are you?" Asaph was in the tension of belief and unbelief. While the appearance of God's lack of action seems like a failure on God's part, faith calls me to trust God anyway. Like Job's anguish, my grief limits my perspective, and I think I understand the fullness of God's activity. However, the truth of Scripture and God's character reveal God's will has not failed me, but He has allowed me to experience deep grief. Although this grief is not welcomed by me, God is with me as I live in the shadow of grief. A theology of grief allows us to admit that both God is good and faithful, and great grief exist at the same time; this is our starting point to understanding grief from God's perspective.

Asaph confessed God was doing something. "You kept my eyes from closing; I was too troubled to speak" (verse 4, NIV). The closed eyelids are the outward evidence of an inward broken heart. Asaph was seeking comfort and not receiving it. In a commentary from the late 1800s, Alexander Maclaren wrote a powerful description of those who know grieve,

> *Sorrow, like a beast of prey, devours at night; and every sad heart knows how eyelids, however wearied, refuse to close upon as wearied eyes, which gaze wide opened into the blackness and see dreadful things there. This man felt as if God's finger was pushing up his lids and forcing him to stare out into the night.*[11]

God was forcing Asaph to face his grief; this led Asaph to question God's love and faithfulness. God is not obliged to provide an escape from the grief, as to quickly return life to a normalcy after the loss of a loved one would be a dishonor to the person who passed. There may be some people who want to solely focus on celebrating the "life after death" that they fail to acknowledge the life on earth will be missed by many. As followers of Jesus, we look forward to the resurrection, but we must live in the moment of loss, therefore God's perspective of grief is to *live focused on both*. Grieve with the hope of Heaven as our reality (1 Thessalonians 4:13; Philippians 3:20–21), but grieve—fully grieve, with tears facing our loss. We grieve knowing God is grieving with us. The tears of Jesus, shed alongside the family and friends of Lazarus (John 11:35), is evidence that it is right to mourn and grieve.

---

[11] Alexander Maclaren, *The Psalms,* Volume 2: Psalms 39–89 (Hodder and Stoughton, 1892).

Debbie's Journey

My perspective on grief has completely changed from earlier in my life. I encountered loss as a young child with loss of my maternal grandparents and observing my mother grieve and mourn for her parents. This opened my curiosity to depression and mental health. I realized that we all grieve so differently from one another and that no one should be judged on how they chose to grieve. Looking back, I admire my mother more now than I ever did as I remember her in a deep depression after her mother passed away. My mother quickly learned about self-care alongside her spiritual and intimate time with the Lord.

Asaph finished this section of lament in verse 9 by again giving a *Selah*, allowing the congregation time to reflect on the pressing question most people ask, "Why would a loving God do this?" I have interacted with many people since the passing of Adam who have asked that question, "Why would a loving God do this?" The reality of good-people experiencing bad-things seems to be the greatest roadblock to faith in God. This points to the question of God's sovereignty and humanity's freewill that I don't have the space or intention to fully speak about at this point of my journey. However, let me summarize the doctrine of God's sovereignty: God is continually involved with all created things in such a way that He keeps them existing and directs them to fulfill His purpose, therefore God is sovereign, and nothing can thwart or stop God's will (Ephesians 1:11; Colossians 1:16–17; Isaiah 45:7–9; Proverbs 16:33). Remember from our discussion of Job's journey of faith in times of grieving that Job concluded God is sovereign, "I know that you can do all things; no purpose of yours can be thwarted" (Job 42:2, NIV).

An aspect of the doctrine of God's sovereignty as providence is the doctrine of concurrence, which affirms that God directs, and works through the distinctive properties of each created thing, so these choices bring about the results we see (Proverbs 16:1; Acts 3:13; 4:27–28; Ephesians 1:4). God's predetermined plan and our freewill both exist and work together as God upholds our ability to make willing, responsible choices, that have real and eternal results, for which we are held accountable. This truth allows us to take the "bad things" that happen in our lives, which are the willful choice of others and turn them over to God to work out for His purpose. The biblical story of Joseph and the betrayal of his brothers is an example of God's providence in concurrence with human free will. "But Joseph said to them, 'Don't be afraid. Am I in the place of God? You intended to harm me, but God intended it for good to accomplish what is now being done, the saving of many lives'" (Genesis 50:19–20, NIV). Returning to our question of faith, "Why would a loving God allow...?," God allows pain and suffering for a variety of reasons: some are caused by other people, others by the chance of nature, others are simply just allowed by God. But all circumstances are still within God's ordained plan and bring us back to a brokenness that is only met by God Himself.

Psalm 42 captures what many are feeling in our world when overcome by brokenness, "As the deer longs for streams of water, so I long for you, O God. I thirst for God, the living God. When can I go and stand before him? Day and night I have only tears for food, while my enemies continually taunt me, saying, '*Where is this God of yours?*'" (Psalm 42:1–3, NLT, emphasis added). For those of us who know Jesus as God, Savior, and Lord, we try to remember God's goodness just as the psalmist remembers the good times but comes back to his pain and grief "'O God my rock,' I cry, 'Why have you forgotten me? Why must I wander around in grief, oppressed by my enemies?' Their taunts break my bones. They scoff, '*Where is this God of yours?*'"

(Psalm 42:9–10, NLT, emphasis added). You hear a lie long enough and you start to wonder if it is truth. Notice the repetition in this psalm that our hardship and grief lead others to think there is no God ("Where is this God of yours?"), but we know differently—we know God is with us in the grief and suffering of loss.

The chorus of Psalm 42 is a vow of praise—repeated twice—and is the final thought of the psalm, "Why am I discouraged? Why is my heart so sad? I will put my hope in God! I will praise him again—my Savior and my God!" (verses 5 and 11, NLT). This statement is a willful statement of trust that is thrust into the midst of grief and doubt. It is a statement that God is still good, that God is still MY God! The Bible never fully answers WHY God allows suffering. The good news is God did not intend for life to be like this; and He promises to be with us in the pain. This leads to an understanding of God's perspective of grief, that because God is with us in the pain, He can purpose the pain for good. Scripture says God can use the pain to build perseverance and resilience in us. "I consider that our present sufferings are not worth comparing with the glory that will be revealed in us … We know that the whole creation has been groaning as in the pains of childbirth right up to the present time" (Romans 8:18, 22, NIV). These verses offer hope but not immediate relief! Grief will impact your faith, but it does not have to destroy your faith. Even the faith of saints who suffered in the past, lived their lives built upon the bedrock of God's truth displaying His faithfulness, goodness, and sovereignty. Grief has a way of stripping away the scaffolding of religion that we have surrounded ourselves with to reveal bare what we truly believe, holding onto what you know to be true regardless of your circumstances and the shadow of grief.

Debbie's Journey

Grief sucks! It pulls you into a place where you are forced to question what you believe and what is real. It also affects your being in ways you cannot anticipate. I am trying to implement rest and solitude time to recover from days full of triggers of losing Adam.

The last truth about God's perspective of grief I want to highlight is that grief is ultimately temporary. The long shadow of grief has changed us in some ways but ultimately there will be a moment when we no longer grieve. That moment may come to some one day on earth, but all followers of Jesus can be assured their grief will end in the Resurrection.

> *Then I saw "a new heaven and a new earth," for the first heaven and the first earth had passed away, and there was no longer any sea. I saw the Holy City, the new Jerusalem, coming down out of heaven from God, prepared as a bride beautifully dressed for her husband. And I heard a loud voice from the throne saying, "Look! God's dwelling place is now among the people, and he will dwell with them. They will be his people, and God himself will be with them and be their God. 'He will wipe every tear from their eyes.* **There will be no more death' or mourning or crying or pain**, *for the old order of things has passed away"* (Revelation 21:1–4, NIV, emphasis added).

I am on a journey of faith in Jesus like many of you. I believe my Savior Jesus suffered death in my place to atone for my sins. I believe Jesus physically arose from the dead with the same power of God that now lives in me; this is my eternal hope that as He is I will be. I live fully confident that God will deliver me after death to be united with Him and all the saints in Heaven—especially my son Adam. This journey of faith has its ups and downs; days filled with grief and an aching questioning of God and other days with His grace and mercy showering me with His peaceful presence. I still live in the tension of believing Jesus is enough and wondering why God did not do more to spare my son. Yet I seek to daily follow Jesus, trusting despite my temporary feelings, He is always with me.

SUMMARY OF GOD'S PERSPECTIVE OF GRIEF:

1. God in His faithfulness and great grief do exist at the same time and place.
2. We can grieve with hope because of the reality of Heaven.
3. It is right to grieve as Jesus grieved the earthly death of loved ones.
4. God is with us in the pain and suffering of grief.
5. God can purpose the pain of grief for good.
6. Grief will come to an end.

CHAPTER 6
CIRCLE THE WAGONS

YOU CAN'T DO THIS ALONE

When Adam passed away, I was overwhelmed by all the "things" I had to do. The list was actually very small, but it felt suffocating. We had a memorial to plan. We had to meet with the mortuary. Phone calls to make to the Coroner's office to understand what caused his death. Funds to raise to help Adam's wife and soon-to-be-born child. My church gave us time off to be with my family. Biola had just begun its summer break. I was "given" time and the expectations on me were minimal, but I felt the weight of each day's decisions.

We relocated to be close to Adam's wife for a few weeks to focus on our primary task of grieving. We spent each day remembering Adam. Sharing pictures. Listening to music. Planning the memorial service. Those first days were actually the easiest as many people sought to take care of our physical needs. It was the looming "what's next?" thoughts that kept me up at night. I've never had a dream about Adam as my wife did. My nightly thoughts were of his family left behind. The weight within me continued to build.

After Adam's memorial, our family decided to continue with our planned vacation to Maui. It was Adam's favorite resort, but he was not included in the plans. He was expecting his first child, and his wife could not fly. However, he was missed like he was supposed to be there, with us, the whole time. I saw Adam in a child playing in the pool. I saw Adam in a young dad holding a baby. I grieved what I would never have—a complete family celebrating each other. As painful as the week in Maui was, it also provided a chance for our family to come together, to remember Adam, to seek healing.

On the Hawaiian island we all got temporary henna tattoos in honor of Adam. Mine was simple. Just his initials and "Romans 5:8" intersecting in the form of a cross on my left forearm. It would be the precursor of the full sleeve I have on my left arm to honor Adam. We returned home from Maui just in time for Adam's daughter to be born. I returned home making a vow to Adam, to care for both his legacy and his family. The weight of responsibilities was now overwhelming me. I felt them. I buckled under the pressure. Panic in the sadness is the best I could describe what I was feeling.

Prolonged sadness results in an elevated anxiousness and sense of panic. The same methods used to address the panic attacks in Critical Incident Stress Management, associated with traumatic events experienced by first responders and the like, are relevant to dealing with the stress of grief. One practice that I have helped facilitate for others in the fire service to fend off the panic attacks is called a debriefing. This is an intentional gathering of all the personnel who were involved in a tragic call's response to come and share their experiences. Trained counselors ask willing participates to share what they saw, did, and experienced. Not every person has to share, simply hearing the perspective of others is helpful in bringing a sense of closure to this event. Often the stoic first responders sit silently until an older member of the department breaks with emotion, relating this tragic event to others he has endured. This starts the emotional outpouring of others who have now been given permission to feel the full weight of their stress associated with this tragic event they witnessed. This is not the end of the healing process; it is actually just the beginning for those who have been adversely affected by the trauma. The key is to notice how it began; it began in a circle. The circle of chairs with people listening to each other, supporting each other, filling in gaps of knowledge, and simply crying together. They "circled the wagons" and the healing was allowed to begin.

Looking back, I now recognize the intentional "circling of the wagons" that our family did. This phrase, "circle the wagons," is an old western pioneer term. As the wagon trains head out west, following the rutted trails of those who had gone before them, when the day's journey was over the single-file line of wagons would make a circle for protection. The cooking, mending, and daily business would take place within the circle of wagons. Some larger wagons would circle up to corral the cattle during the evening hours. This formation of the wagons also provided protection from the external threats of the wild frontier. The call to "circle the wagons" could be announced at any moment there was a sense of danger.

In today's culture ethos, "circling the wagons" is used figuratively to describe the action by a group of people to protect against an attack or to unite against or for a common cause. While some may see negative historical undertones of this posture, the turning inward to those closest to you is a trusted formation. In sports' terminology, it's the team huddle, with arms wrapped around each other, listening closely to one another. This was the formation that our family took to unite with key individuals we allowed in our circle to grieve at the intense level we were grieving. It was a small circle that most did not want to be part of due to the amount of pain shouldered by those in the circle.

TO THOSE REACTING TO GRIEF: "WHO'S IN YOUR CIRCLE?"

So, who is allowed in the "circle"? This is an important question. Too small and you will not experience the protection required during this season of grieving. Too big and you will be overwhelmed with requests and others needing attention from you. We limited the circle to those who "had" to be present: immediate family impacted and very close extended family members and friends who knew their role was to grieve alongside us. While there are many needs at the first moments of loss, both physical and spiritual, it is the emotional need to simply be present together and grieve in each person's unique way that is important. If someone feels the need to provide care in arranging meals or take care of other physical needs, that is an indicator this person is not in the immediate circle with you, as this circle cannot do much more than simply be together.

There were many people who loved us deeply and were tools God used to sustain us during those first few weeks, taking care of our physical and emotional needs; to list them all would be a disservice to all those countless people who prayed, cared, gave food, gave money, gave us space to grieve who will never be rightly named. As I look back on our response to grief, I see the "concentric circles" of people supporting us. Each circle of people served in, and continue to fulfill, specific roles of strength-giving care and tangible help. There are three distinct circles, surrounding our immediate inner family-circle, that we needed as we responded in grief to the loss of Adam. Let me explain these roles to insure you begin to assemble your circles of support.

CIRCLE #1: "AARON AND HUR"

To say Debbie and I could not have survived the loss of Adam without the love and extended care from many people would not be an overstatement. Debbie and I were not enough for each other, and we could never be. We could not breath. We could not even drive ourselves to be with Adam in those first moments of grief. We fell into the arms of close friends and family members. Our immediate family: our daughter, son, Adam's wife, could not be this first circle of support. We were all too broken. While we held onto to each other in what may have appeared to be a circle, functioning as one body—we were failing under the weight of intense pain. We needed others to become our first circle of care. We have already credited our "five-minute friends," Jake and Shelli, for their sacrificial gifts to us of time, doing for us what we could not do for ourselves. However, even they were not enough. In many ways they were one half of the "Aaron and Hur" combo team that Moses needed to support him through crisis.

Scripture records a battle between the Israelites and the Amalekites in Exodus 17 in which God empowered the Israelites to win the battle as long as Moses lifted up his hands in prayer, holding an ever-increasing heavy staff high in the air. "As long as Moses held up his hands, the Israelites were winning, but whenever he lowered his hands, the Amalekites were winning" (Exodus 17:11, NIV). This was the first significant experience of warfare the Israelites encountered after they left Egypt. The Amalekites had raided the Israelites by attacking the rear group of the people, the weakest of the clan, to take their treasures, and in the process killing the women, children, and elderly, not the warriors who were at the front of the travel party. Deuteronomy 25 described the method of attack, "Remember what the Amalekites did to you along the way when you came out of Egypt. When you were weary and worn out, they met you on your journey and attacked all who were lagging behind; they had no fear of God" (verses 17–18, NIV). Moses trusted God for victory and interceded on the hilltop for the warriors in battle below (Exodus 17:10).

As Moses prayed God gave victory to the Israelites, but Moses tired as the battle continued late into the day. Therefore, Moses' brother Aaron and the community leader Hur, came to stand beside him and hold up his arms, one on each side of Moses. "When Moses' hands grew tired, they took a stone and put it under him and he sat on it. Aaron and Hur held his hands up—one on one side, one on the other—so that his hands remained steady till sunset. So Joshua overcame the Amalekite army with the sword" (Exodus 17:12–13, NIV). The result was not just victory but a powerful example of the role we can play in another person's life as we are enduring struggles in life.

The qualities each of these men possessed are important to note as these enabled them to come alongside to support Moses in his time of need. First, Aaron and Hur demonstrated a long-standing commitment to Moses. Aaron was present with Moses in the very beginning of the campaign to free the Israelites from Egypt, first mentioned in Exodus 4. "Then the Lord's anger burned against Moses and he said, "What about your brother, Aaron the Levite? I know he can speak well. He is already on his way to meet you, and he will be glad to see you … He will speak to the people for you, and it will be as if he were your mouth and as if you were God to him" (Exodus 4:14, 16, NIV). Together Moses and Aaron worked together through the initial struggles and plagues to bring about God's miraculous deliverance from slavery. Aaron was not perfect, and faltered greatly at the end of his life, but in key moments Aaron had shown faithfulness to his brother Moses, and that long lasting commitment brought Aaron to that hilltop to pray alongside and lift up Moses' arms for victory.

We are not told much about Hur. However, Jewish tradition implies Hur was Moses' brother-in-law.[12] While Aaron was a known spiritual leader of the community; Hur was a family member who cared deeply for Moses and took on the servant role of physically meeting a need for Moses—holding up his arms in prayer. This is the second quality needed for this most inner circle: a servant's heart to do whatever is needed. If Jake was my "Aaron," Phil was my "Hur." Phil was a relatively new friend at church. Debbie and I joined a Bible study at his and his wife's house. Phil and I were becoming close friends when Adam died. Phil was at a loss of what to do and say. He wrestled with his own emotions having never met Adam but grieving all the same for me as a dad and a friend who had just lost a child. He could not imagine my pain, but he also did not try. Phil simply allowed me to grieve with him as he silently lifted me up in prayer. In the months after Adam passed away, as other people were returning to "normalcy," Phil would allow me to simply sit in his pool, sometimes all by myself, other times he would join me. In those moments, he sent his kids inside, even though they too wanted to swim; Phil created the space where I could simply be honest and raw with my emotions and doubts. Phil wrestled with his own thoughts and feelings, trying hard not to make things worse, so many times he would simply sit, occasionally asking a question. That is the role of a servant, to simply be present awaiting instructions of how to help. For Moses,

[12] Frank E. Gaebelein, gen. ed., *The Expositor's Bible Commentary: Genesis, Exodus, Leviticus, Numbers* Volume 2 (Zondervan, 1990), 408.

Hur needed to hold up an arm. For me, Phil needed to sit in a pool and simply be present.

There was third person playing a vital role in this battle, Joshua. This battle is the first time we read of Joshua's leadership. Joshua was in the thick of fighting for his people. This is the third characteristic of the first circle, they are willing to battle for you. This first circle of friends became a line of defense for Debbie and me, creating the healing space by establishing firm boundaries that prevented intruders from invading the sacredness of our grief. This first circle took care of our home as we were gone for weeks to be with Adam's wife. This first circle ran interference for us with those who were curious as to our wellbeing. This first circle did what needed to be done, regardless of the "thanks" or glamour of the role.

Your first circle will probably be more than two people, more than just Aaron and Hur, but it probably will self-limit itself to four individuals or couples. In your state of grief, you will not be able to extend yourself to more people than this. However, the key is not the number of people but rather the qualities they possess. Without the commitment, servanthood, and willingness to battle for us, the road of grief would have been much harder for Debbie and me.

Debbie's Journey

My first circle was like Dave's as I leaned on my "bestie" Shelli the most. She cared for me as a best friend should. Shelli and Jake had us over every week for dinner when we were able to dine with them one year into our grief. This first circle included calls and texts and visits from my spiritual daughter Ashley and my cousin Diane. These three women were my troop! My troop protected me, challenged me, loved me ,and were my prayer warriors!

CIRCLE #2: "TRUSTED CONFIDANTS"

Circle number two is a difficult circle to navigate because often these individuals feel they should be included in the first circle of care. However, for any number of reasons, it is best to consider them in the still very important, but not as involved, circle number two. While these individuals may express disappointment they are not included more, it is important to recognize these individuals are trusted confidants whose support is very necessary.

Trusted confidants are those people you choose to share the emotional weight of grief with in small, bite-size pieces. The description was intentionally written to identify key characteristics of circle number two people: you choose who they are and what to share with them. In other words, circle number two is on a "need-to-know" status, waiting for the moments that you are ready to share with them, seeking new perspectives. Circle number two individuals must be willing to wait and not pressure you for more time or information, and you may need to remind these people you know they are to be willing and available for when the time is right for you. Debbie and I have three types of people in our circle number two, all very important and loved by us.

Extended Family Members

First, it is important to remember your extended family is grieving deeply as well. Adam was the first grandchild my mom lost, the first nephew my sisters had to say "goodbye" to. The history that your extended family had with your loved one who passed away will provide beautiful stories to remember. There will be time to gather and remember together. Your extended family members will have different memories and experiences you will not be aware of, therefore, extended family members are helpful in the grieving process as you will discover new and wonderful aspects of your loved one's life to be celebrated. These stories may cause you to ask questions and seek new perspectives about your journey with grief. The faith of these extended family members will be an important extension of your faith, as your weakness is yoked together with them to help sustain you. You can vent frustrations and pain to these extended family members because they are committed to you, regardless of the circumstances. These extended family members will remain silent when needed and speak truth when you will need to be reminded of it. Not all family members can handle this load, which is why only some extended family members will be allowed in circle number two: trusted confidants.

Extended family members are also in a position to give more resources than most people. Debbie's cousin Diane and her husband Mike literally gave us their home for a few weeks so we could be near Adam's wife and not have to live in a hotel in those first moments of extreme grief. They stocked their refrigerator with simple foods, easy to cook. Adam's in-laws opened their home daily to us to join Adam's wife, again giving us the space to simply be. The common theme for all of these responses from extended family members is they were simply available to us, offering us tangible support that we could take or leave, no obligations to give more of ourselves in exchange. Not all extended family members can function in this way, which excludes them from being in circle number two. You must have others who can run interference with these overbearing family members, and who better than another extended family member who is a trusted confidant.

Other Close Friends

There will be friendships that will be greatly affected by the loss of your loved one. People who love you and your whole family that are deeply hurting. At Adam's funeral, Debbie and I were overwhelmed by the pain people were experiencing, many needing a hug from us. We get it, we were all hurting. Adam was beloved by so many people from many different contexts, his memorial was a mosaic of beautiful people with the pain in their heart uniting them. I share this because, while all these people were grieving with us, only a few other couples were allowed into circle number two. The key was they put their needs on the "back burner," not pressing for time with us or closure for their own emotions.

Our good friend Harley is a prime example of this. Harley and her husband served with us at church. We love hanging out with them and their young kids. Harley took the lead of organizing meals to be dropped off at our house for our family once we returned from vacation. Many people wanted to give, so the organization was a large task, which Harley did admirably. The reason Harley is a great example of close friends in circle number two is she waited for us to engage with her; even though she was daily serving us, she did not insist on having time with us until we were ready. Other people came over unannounced, trying to give us things, seeking a moment of our time. We often never opened the door to those people. However, when we were ready, there was a day when Harley came over with her kids to drop off food and we opened the door to run after her to give a big hug. We wanted her to know how important she was to us, how loved we felt by her actions. We were ready to express ourselves to her and she was willing to receive us. Soon after that, we went to her house to spend time with her family. This was made possible because Harley, our close friend, was willing to go by our terms.

"Other close friends" will not feel as they are being treated as a close friend because their access to you has changed. I am sad to admit that Debbie and I lost friends during this time because people thought they deserved to be included in circle number one or two, and for a variety of reasons, they were left out. We are so grateful for the close friends who waited and waited until we were ready. Some of our friends waited over a year to reengage with us, and we are very thankful they were willing to wait. These friends are trusted confidants because they trusted us to know what we needed and trusted that we would ask them when we needed it.

Counselors

Lastly, you will need wise counselors in this season. Our family had multiple and varying types of counselors we sought out in our journey with grief. We had a family counselor for Debbie, Mfundo, and I to meet with. Each of us had individual counseling. I changed counselors a few times in the process. The hardship in the selection of a counselor is knowing what you need in that moment from the counseling session. Those needs are ever changing and unique to you, and potentially different from your spouse. In the beginning I did not know what I needed and therefore, my closest friends became my counselors. As the journey with grief continued, I realized I needed help enduring the "Shadow of Grief" and found a counselor who was able to ask me insightful questions to move into expanding my capacity to grieve with hope. I have altered the frequency of my counseling sessions as I have experienced different seasons of life, taking breaks altogether when I felt I had a reached a plateau in the process and resuming when new self-awareness showed a renewed need for counsel. I share with you my journey with counseling, which has been different from Debbie's, to give you permission to seek counseling as you determine your need and receptivity to counseling. Change the person and frequency until you find the right situation. Some people seek group therapy in ministries such as "Grief Share"; I have participated in a few grief groups but have found the most meaningful perspectives from the individual counseling sessions. A good counselor is worth the investment, even if you must spend your own money because the right counselor for you is not covered by your insurance. If this is the case, ask the counselor if they will see you for less money on a "sliding scale." You must find your own way in this important resource in circle number two; who is a trusted confidant for you?

Debbie's Journey

My second circle overlaps with Dave's. I am still brought to tears thinking of the generosity of my cousins Mike and Diane and Adam's in-laws. I will forever be grateful for how they housed us and fed us. My Mom, the most trusted prayer warrior of my life, was so heartbroken she could barely speak to me but still would remind me she was praying for me until she passed two years after Adam. My Dad passed away very quickly, four months after Adam did. These losses have been not just challenging to my extended family but especially hard blows to my remaining children. I will always be grateful for close friends such as Harley and her family and the love they give. My counselor Karen could be included in other circles but will only be mentioned last in this circle because she was so intricate in the first months of my grief. She helped me navigate grief and mourning and taught me how to do this in a healthy way. She is and will always be my faithful counselor.

CIRCLE #3: "COMMUNITY OF FAITH"

The last circle of care is the larger community of faith in your context. This should include your church but can also include other Christians you know, as well as other churches. The death of Adam intimately impacted five churches: the church where he served, the three churches I served at, and a church that my former students recently planted. Each of these churches were grieving the loss of Adam in their own unique way. Adam was their youth pastor. The kid they remember growing up. The child of a beloved pastor. Debbie and I are so grateful to Adam's senior pastor, Pastor John, who cared so deeply for our family. Grace Church Glendora became our church too in that moment. The people of God that we championed from afar as Adam served them were now necessary to help us grieve rightly. This church took on key responsibilities for Adam's memorial service and food for our family in those first days of grieving. Our local church where I pastor was an incredible source of strength as they gathered spontaneously in prayer for our family the day Adam died. Our church served our physical needs as well as gave us room to grieve. They respected our wishes to be present in worship without singing and held back from hugs we were not able to receive.

The Church is more than a building, it's more than a gathering of people to worship God. The Church is the family of God that has mutual obligation toward one another. "But God has put the body together, giving greater honor to the parts that lacked it, so that there should be no division in the body, but that its parts should have equal concern for each other. If one part suffers, every part suffers with it; if one part is honored, every part rejoices with it" (1 Corinthians 12:24–26, NIV). When the local church is functioning rightly, each person is loved and known, including their griefs and joys, because of the equal concern shown. This Greek word for *concern* (verse 25) is the same word we translate "worry," such as in Matthew 6.[13] The context of 1 Corinthians 12 informs us that this word should be held as a positive action, not the negative as "do not worry." It would be right to say the church is to be righteously anxious for one another, meeting the needs as we can for each other. This includes the need for space as well as the need for meals during the time of grief. Most of us struggle to "not worry" as Matthew 6 commands us; what would our community of faith be like if we place that same energy into prayerfully thinking of each other's needs first? I believe the result would be a church to seek to be for each other what the other person truly needs—a circle of care.

However, when the church members are focused on their own personal needs, the local gathering can be a place of unwarranted pain and well-meaning but inappropriate words and action. To those of you who have been wounded in your time of grief by others in your church, don't let the missteps of some keep you from joining God's design for spiritual care; I strongly encourage you to embrace your local community of faith again.

Debbie's Journey

The third circle is our community of faith. The people of God coming together to grieve alongside you, to help in tangible ways. This was shown to us in so many facets that I can't recall each. Yes, there were loving and good ways many stepped up to grieve with us at the same time there were not so loving words shared with us and at us. In this shadow of grief there will be positive and negative

[13] Strong's Lexicon, "G3309 – *merimnaō*," https://www.blueletterbible.org/lexicon/g3309/kjv/tr/0-1/.

experiences. I must remind myself to focus on what the Word of God says and how we are to treat one another in anyone's time of grief. I urge you, reader, to do the same.

TO THOSE WALKING ALONGSIDE SOMEONE IN GRIEF

To the church and those of you who care enough about someone who is grieving to read this book, thank you for your desire to help. Thank you for the time and resources you have given. Thank you for your concern but please be patient with those who are grieving by following these three pieces of guidance.

WAIT TO BE INVITED IN

First, as discussed previously, please wait until the person grieving invites you to join in their journey with grief. It is not about you. If you are grieving, then grieve with your circles of care. Your pain is not an excuse to intrude where you have not been invited. As you wait, pray—pray for yourself, pray for those hurting, pray for God's strength to sustain you in the waiting.

ASK AND THEN WAIT

While this may seem contradictory, it is appropriate to text or write a note letting the grieving person know that you care for them and are sorry for this loss. Do not take offense if the person doesn't respond to you, they may not have the emotional bandwidth to do anything in the moment. If you send a text or write a note, wait three weeks, and if no response still, send another note simply stating you are praying for them. Keep the note simple. Even if no response, just know everyone likes to hear people are praying for them. Remember to make this about the other person, so don't have expectations of a response or inclusion that the other person may not be able to give.

ONCE YOU OFFER HELP, BE PREPARED TO FOLLOW THROUGH

Lastly, if you offer help at any point, be ready to honor that offer, whenever the other person is ready for the help. Most people want to help in the crisis. Many people offered to help Adam's wife and my family, however in the moment there was nothing we wanted or needed from them. Yet weeks later, when help was needed, these individuals were no longer available. This added more pain to the situation as it reinforced the isolation that we found ourselves in. Therefore, it may be best not to offer any help and wait until a request is made for something specific.

I hope you have picked up on the theme of waiting to respond. Waiting is a very caring act as it elevates the person in pain to be the priority, not our need to be needed and useful. Waiting does not have to be passive though. Waiting allows for deeper times of prayer. Waiting matures our motives to be Christ-honoring and other-focused. Waiting brings people together to wait and even focuses their energy on other tasks the grieving person may never know. Use the time to organize a fund raiser and give the money to the family in the form a gift card that can be used at multiple retailers or restaurants. Organize a workday to finish yard work and house projects that have sat idle (suggestion: arrange for the family to be gone that day to give them the privacy they need). The point is that waiting is not doing nothing, it is just doing different things based on the true needs of the person who is living in the shadow of grief.

CHAPTER 7

GRIEVING DIFFERENTLY

GRIEVE AUTHENTICALLY

It is sad to admit but there were some who judged Debbie and I in our grief. They rarely voiced their opinion to us—those who did often caused more pain than necessary. However, we knew people were forming impressions of what a "good Christian" would do in times of death, because God declares "precious in the sight of the LORD is the death of his faithful servants (Psalm 116:15, NIV). These impressions created a tension within Debbie and I to grieve in "publicly acceptable ways," which meant to grieve as they would approve of the grieving process. The truth is even Debbie and I disagreed and differed with each other on how we should be grieving. But that was okay.

There are various factors that will impact how we grieve. Some of those factors, such as gender and culture, are "hardwired" into our thinking, shaping how we process and express emotions. Therefore, a husband and wife will often grieve differently from one another. Neither is wrong in their grief response, just different as we must remember everyone's experience to grief is different. Debbie and I did not follow normal gender styles of grieving. According to psychologists, men have grown up in a society in which crying may be viewed as a sign of weakness. Our movie heroes demonstrate men rise to action; they do not remain in an emotional state. This places a pressure upon men "to be strong and independent [that] might limit displays of emotion or avoid talking about their feelings."[14] This limiting of emotions may cause a man to move more quickly through the emotional response to engage in "normalcy" again. The coping mechanisms for men usually bring men to activity: caring for family needs, looking for a distraction in some work project, or even working more at their job to create a sense of financial security for the family.

I was a combination of these factors. It took me a full day before I legitimately broke down and sobbed. I was controlling my emotions for the sake of my family who were in deep grief immediately. I thought about how I needed to take care of Adam's wife and soon-to-be born daughter. I rallied others to financial support of his family. I moved quickly into planning Adam's memorial service. I needed to be with others. One of the first groups I started hanging around with were the firefighters that I was the chaplain for. These men and women knew my story and expressed deep concern for me and my family as they daily witness other families devastated by some type

---

[14] St. Jude Hospital, "Gender Differences in the Grieving Process," *St. Jude Together* (August 2023).

of crisis. While this has not made them counseling experts, it did prepare them to be present in the awkwardness of grief. While many people try to avoid dealing with painful situations, these firefighters turned toward the "fire" in my life and were present. In similar ways, I wanted to return quickly to our small group from church. However, this did not happen as Debbie was much different from me in her grieving response.

Debbie's Journey

Grieving as a follower of Jesus is not spoken about as much as it should. There will always be ways people grieve differently than you. Just that fact alone should make it a bit easier to extend grace when someone is in their own deep grief. I did grieve differently from Dave straight from the beginning. My first reactions to losing my son were uncontrollable sobbing and groaning. Prayer came almost immediately after for me. Prayer has always been where I go in chaos. This loss was unique and hit me with a heavy blow, which led to some difficult days ahead. I also needed clarity/a making sense of what just happened. I then hurt for my daughter in law and soon to be born granddaughter, and then I turned to solitude.

Not all women will be like Debbie. Women in general are more likely to express grief with others. However, this ability to express grief with others does not lead to an automatic sense of understanding. Mothers who have lost a child may feel other mothers have trouble sharing how they truly feel. This can lead to a woman feeling angry or resentful when others cannot join them in their level of pain. This is even true for a married couple. Both partners have lost a child, but they express their grief differently. This difference causes increased tension in a marriage as it may lead one spouse to question the relationship with their spouse if they are unable to share their grief and work through it together, assuming the other spouse doesn't care. "One spouse may find it more difficult to express grief openly, the other may be very emotional, and possibly resent the other for not 'caring as much.' … Many times, you may expect each other to relieve the pain for each other and when this doesn't happen, you can begin to feel angry, resentful, hurt, or abandoned …."[15] The reality is they do care—they just care and grieve differently.

WAYS PEOPLE GRIEVE DIFFERENTLY

We briefly touched on some of the ways men and women will grieve differently. The multiple cultural variations of grief are tied to specific beliefs about death and the afterlife. For the Christian, the Scriptures of our faith that give us hope in our grief—hope of everlasting life that continues after physical death (John 3:16); however, we will still grieve in demonstrably different ways. This does not negate our hope but rather are important expressions of grief that must be released and not "bottled up" for the sake of respectability.

WE WILL GRIEVE DIFFERENTLY IN THREE IMPORTANT ASPECTS:

Our Emotions: Sudden and unexpected loss will cause many people to feel extreme sadness. Some will express this sadness in verbal or physical displays. Others will become silent, numb to the world,

[15] Carolina Counseling Services, "Protecting Your Marriage Against the Impact of Grief" https://sanfordnccounseling.carolinacounselingservices.com/protecting-your-marriage-against-the-impact-of-grief/.

keeping their emotions within themselves. If the death was the final act of a prolonged illness, a person may feel relieved, having already grieved the loss long ago. All these emotional responses can be appropriate for the person and therefore, we should not judge someone who has a different emotional response than you may to the death of a loved one.

How we express love to one another can also play a role in how we express our emotions of grief. For those of us, like myself, who crave verbal affirmations, we will speak our emotions for the loss and of our love for the person. When my father passed away many years ago, I wanted to speak at the service on behalf of the family to express my gratitude toward others and my admiration of my dad. My mom did not want to speak or have a letter read from her; she simply made a bouquet of flowers for the funeral to express how she felt. She said "He knows..." as her love language of acts of service was an expression of her emotional state of heart and mind.

Emotional regulation is a developmental task that affects much of our life from early childhood and on. "It appears that both attachment styles and emotion regulation are factors that influence the trajectory of one's bereavement."[16] The response to trauma is impacted by the ability to make healthy attachments based on trust. Sudden grief breaks that trust and impacts the emotional regulation of a person, causing them to act differently than we would expect. Again, each different grief response requires a loving patience to bring about healing in its due time.

---

[16] W. Katzman, & N. Papouchis, "Grief Responses during the COVID-19 Pandemic: Differences in Attachment and Emotion Regulation," Journal of Loss & Trauma, 27(8), (2022): 761–772, 763.

Mode: This leads to a second difference in people's grief—the communal modality in which people grieve. People may express grief openly, in private, or through actions like journaling. We have described grief as an iceberg. What you see "above the water line," expressed in community, is a small portion of the grief a person is dealing with. The mode of grief expressions does not diminish the level of pain or sincerity of the emotion. We should keep to ourselves the assumptions we make about someone who is grieving, regardless of how they are outwardly enduring the season of loss. The challenge with those who grieve in an outward modality is the awkwardness of bringing other people into their pain. This unwanted "invitation" is tolerated for a moment, almost expected, which creates concern for those who grieve in private. We become worried that they are a "ticking time bomb" that will explode creating emotional and relational damage. It is as if the person experiencing sudden grief is in a "no-win" situation regardless the mode they choose to express their deep pain.

Focus: People may focus on the loss or on restoration. Some people are future-centered, so their thoughts immediately go to what is coming. This focus of grief will become a source of strength for the person as they focus on the hope of Heaven or the steps of rebuilding the means of security (financial, relational) for their "new season" of life. Other people need to reflect deeply on the loss of the person, longing to keep any aspect of the person "alive" with them. The "moving on" of others will be offensive to the person who is focused on the loss. While this person knows life will be different, they are not ready for the demands of this "different season" of life. Each person needs grace and mercy. The person who is focused on restoration may move too fast and cause pain in the wake of their movements. This person needs our support to take the steps they desire with minimal judgment. The person who wants to linger a little longer in grieving the loss needs our grace of space to allow them to mourn appropriately. Both responses can become unhealthy and there will be a time to speak "truth in love" into the situation, but we can patiently be with the person with either focus, praying for God's work to bring the person through this season of grief.

TO THOSE IN THE SHADOW OF GRIEF

GRIEVE AUTHENTICALLY

As you have read over the previous paragraphs, you probably noticed one or two ways you grieve differently from other people. You are grieving this way because you are a unique creation of God, His workmanship, created in His image (Genesis 1:26–27; Ephesians 2:10). Your situation is different from everyone else's. The relationship you had to the one who passed away is unique and special. The dependency you had upon them was different. The expectations of what the future would have been with that person are different. Knowing all these realities of how unique you are in your grief, why would you expect to grieve like anyone else? Why would you allow others to pressure you to conform to their "picture" of grieving well? Debbie and I want you to hear that above many of these lessons—you need to be authentic in how you grieve, because only then will you be able to move forward in healing and restoration.

Debbie's Journey

In my own solace and privacy is how I grieved the most. This is where I retreated after trying to be around others like Dave needed. It was a failed attempt, which I of course expected because I knew to be around certain people would just cause me more pain. Though I would resort to grieve in isolation, I still needed others who knew me well enough to check in with me. I am grateful for my troops whom I mentioned once before. These ladies were my source of help, and every time I reached out, they were there without judgment. These troops allowed me to grieve in my authentic way just as my husband Dave did for me. Dave and I continue to grieve in our own unique ways, and we encourage others to be authentic in their grief.

To grieve authentically, you will need to surround yourself with people who give you the physical and emotional space to grieve as you need to. This will mean some relationships may come to an end as that person will be "toxic" in their burdensome expectations of you. This will add to the grief process but in this immediate response to grief you cannot worry about that now. Later there may be a time for reconciliation, but that's for later. Instead focus on what you need to be and do, and who will be privileged to join you in your unique journey with grief.

REMEMBER YOU ARE NOT ALONE IN YOUR GRIEF

Allow others to grieve alongside you, even if they grieve differently than you are. This may sound counterproductive to the first discussion point we just covered, but the truth is you are not alone in your grief, even if it feels that way. To allow others to grieve alongside you will be challenging. The challenge is not to change how you grieve but to find moments when your grief is similarly experienced. There may be a time of listening to stories being told about the loved one who is no longer physically present; others will remember this person in ways that will complement the memories you have. This is not a time of "I know what you are going through," but rather a time to receive whatever story or expression of grief as a gift of love, time, and thought the other person is offering and consider it a "holy space."

I call you to view your time with other people as "holy space" because we must remember Jesus is at hand. Paul concluded his epistle to the Philippian church by calling the people of God to deal with hardship in a God-focused manner.

> *Rejoice in the Lord always; again I will say, rejoice. Let your reasonableness be known to everyone. The Lord is at hand; do not be anxious about anything, but in everything by prayer and supplication with thanksgiving let your requests be made known to God. And the peace of God, which surpasses all understanding, will guard your hearts and your minds in Christ Jesus* (Philippians 4:4–7, ESV).

We are told to rejoice regardless of our circumstances. This is so difficult to do and, in many ways, can only be done because "Jesus is at hand." I love that phrase. Jesus is present with you! Our response to Jesus being present with us is to rejoice, not because we are in deep pain, but because Jesus is with us in those moments of grieving. Jesus is with me, therefore I can turn to Him in prayer. I take my anxiety about what I've lost and the uncertainty of the future and allow my communion with Him in prayer to change me.

As I prayerfully express gratitude for *who* God is in my pain, grateful that I am not alone in this shadow of grief, I am changed. There is a peace that passes understanding that is the result of truth and hope. This truth is of who Jesus is—the God Almighty, Who is and was and is to come; the Messiah sent by God to redeem and reconcile all of humanity to God. Jesus suffered and grieved the rebellion of the world. He took upon Himself our sin so we could live eternally, as we were originally created, in a resurrected Eden (Heaven) where we will reunite with our loved ones. This our hope—the hope of Heaven. Death was not the end of Jesus' story and therefore, death will not be the end of our story either. Jesus arose from that physical death and burial to a glorified eternity that you and I are invited to join Him in. The truth of Jesus and the hope of Heaven is why we can grieve with hope! For those who know this truth and hope, in the midst of your pain you will experience a form of peace you cannot explain to others, but it will be seen in your countenance, your presence, and your grieving. Jesus is with you, along with others who love you … don't turn your back on them.

Debbie's Journey

Though grief in isolation is where my body and mind wanted to take me, I had to remind myself that staying in isolation is unhealthy. In my prayer times Jesus reminded me through His Scripture that I am not alone. He is always with me even in my grief and He has given me trustworthy women to confide in. Jesus provided in ways I still have trouble explaining, let alone write about. I am so grateful for Dave and how he allows me to speak out about my grief to him in new and colorful ways. Thank you, Lord, for the husband you have given me.

COMMUNICATE WHAT YOU NEED

As you are able, communicate your feelings. Talk to other people honestly about what grief looks and feels like to you. This becomes the common ground that allows others to meet you in your grief and provide you what is most needed in that moment. This will be very difficult at first because you do not know what you need. You will have trouble making decisions in the immediate aftermath of loss. However, try to speak your feelings. Name them. Even if the only words that come to mind are offensive to some—speak them. Do not allow the emotions you have to be bottled up. Those who truly love you will take the verbal "hits" and still return to help. In time you will be able to express what you need, and you should trust those who have remained present with you in the shadow of grief.

FOR THOSE OF YOU WHO ARE WALKING ALONGSIDE SOMEONE IN GRIEF

DO NOT JUDGE THE GRIEF EXPRESSIONS

Scripture gives us some great commands to implement at these moments of people grieving deeply. "Be merciful to those who doubt…" (Jude 1:22, NIV). The unexpected death of a loved one will cause even the strongest Christian to doubt God's loving sovereignty.

My doubts were not the absence of faith but rather a reformation of faith, as I came to a new awareness of how a loving God could allow my greatest pain. We need to be gentle with those who are struggling. Mercy is not giving someone what they deserve. Mercy is withholding judgment, allowing God to work and convict as only God should. If we start with an attitude of mercy, then we can accept the person as they are in this moment as Romans 14 instructs us to do.

> *Accept the one whose faith is weak, without quarreling over disputable matters ... You, then, why do you judge your brother or sister? Or why do you treat them with contempt? For we will all stand before God's judgment seat ... Therefore let us stop passing judgment on one another. Instead, make up your mind not to put any stumbling block or obstacle in the way of a brother or sister* (Romans 14:1, 10, 13, NIV).

Don't cast judgement on the person, don't make things more difficult for the person who is grieving.

HONOR THE OTHER TO GRIEVE DIFFERENTLY

This is the positive action to the command to "stop passing judgment on one another." We refrain from "forcing" each other to act a certain way and instead giving the person the space they need when they want it. We honor the person who is grieving by recognizing the uniqueness of God's image created in them, admitting that they can work out their hope in God differently than you may. Honor says to the other person, "you first." Their needs take priority. Their perspective is given space to be expressed. There will be a time for correction for misdeeds and mistruths that are committed in the aftermath of grief and loss. However, the priority is to accept the person in their weakness and doubt, to love the person as they are—for that is what God is doing.

DO NOT TAKE PERSONALLY A PERSON'S NEGATIVE EMOTIONS

There may be words said to you that are untrue or unkind. Your interests and intentions to help may be rebuffed. You will feel left out at certain moments. None of what is happening will be pleasant, and that is true for all people involved. In the aftermath of the death of a loved one, those most deeply affected will not be able to be concerned about the emotional needs of others. They will only be able to think of their immediate needs. Do not take these actions, statements, and negative expressions personally. Simply respond, "Ok. Maybe another time. Love you." It is natural to be hurt by these negative emotions but take that hurt to someone else who can listen and care for you. Turn your hurt into quick prayers for the person in grief. As you patiently give space for the moment to pass, you may find yourself invited back into the space you desired to be part of previously. While "time" does not heal all wounds, time does allow for new expressions of care to be received. In time, there will be another opportunity to reconnect with the person who is in grief. Wait for that moment.

DOING SMALL ACTS OF KINDNESS OR SERVICE

One way to use this time waiting for an improved relationship is to do small acts of kindness for the person. This could be a random gift card left for them. If you know they have an animal, buy their preferred dog or cat food. When Adam's wife was struggling one day, I took her car and filled it up with gas for her without asking if I could—I just did it. Debbie will buy extra pjs and t-shirts for Adam's daughter so the laundry does not have to be done as frequently. These loving acts are sometimes acknowledged but that's not the point. The point is to make sure Adam's family is cared for, to gently remind Adam's wife she is not alone. The more invasive the service is, the more important to get permission from the person before you do the act of service. Keep seeking the best for the other person, leaving your need for emotional recognition or reciprocal responses for another time.

FINAL WORD FOR THOSE WHO ARE MARRIED

Debbie and I have seen our marriage tested in the shadow of grief and have emerged stronger in our commitment and passion for each other. This did not happen naturally. We were intentional to rebuild from the storm that "blew and beat" against us. We sought help from friends; we sought counseling—both individually and together. I would encourage you to seek marriage counseling if for no other reason than to find common ground and ways to support each other.

> *In grief, there is a profound sense of isolation and there is the tendency to focus on your own feelings, leaving you less energy to devote to others, particularly your spouse. You may not be able to meet all the expectations of your spouse all the time, especially when you are grieving*"[17]

Counseling revealed perspectives that I had assumed about my wife in her grief. Counseling gave us the opportunity to voice our needs and be affirmed these needs were appropriate.

There is a natural drift to pragmatic isolation in marriage due to the demands of family life and away from passion due to: lack of time for each other, lack of energy when we are together, and a lack of creativity after being with each other for years. These factors are compounded by the stress of grief that the couple is now enduring. Debbie

---

[17] Carolina Counseling Services, "Protecting Your Marriage."

and I were determined to lift one another up during our grief, but we also did not want to lose the passion we had spent 30 years enjoying. I have always lived by the motto, "Happy wife, happy life"; Debbie reminds me "Happy spouse, happy house." However you frame it, marriage is about thinking about the other person, but now as you are experiencing grief, there is a third person who has been thrust into your married relationship, the loved one who has died. Grief is the continuation of that love you and your spouse share for the person who died, and it will take energy and time away from your marriage. To regain the passion, Debbie and I intentionally dated each other. That may sound strange for a married couple to go on dates. We had always dated prior to Adam's death, but now in our grief, it was easier to just sit, unengaged with one another. We were stuck in that moment of his death. So we focused on beginning to date again as a precursor to resuming sexual intimacy. Our dates started as walks at the beach, holding hands as we cried and remembered Adam. We expanded our dates to include Disneyland, a favorite place we used to enjoy with our family. We walked around the park, eating and remembering Adam's favorite rides. We found ourselves instinctively laughing together. We found we could have fun still. This was the first clue that our lives moving forward would be lived in the shadow of grief, but they would be full of life nonetheless.

An online post compiling the advice from marriage counselors[18] listed numerous habits of married couples whose marriages last a lifetime; let me give you my top 10 from that list:

---

[18] Kelsey Borresen, "12 Healthy Habits Of Couples Who Are In It For The Long Haul," HuffPost Life, (2022), https://www.huffpost.com/entry/healthy-relationship-habits_l_5c64b-8c7e4b0233af9713b31.

#10 — They are affectionate even outside the bedroom.

#9 — They don't gossip about each other.

#8 — They continually do small things for each other.

#7 — They refuse to play the blame game.

#6 — They set aside time to regularly check in with each other, listening intently before replying.

#5 — They say what they mean and mean what they say.

#4 — They don't make assumptions about their spouse's feelings—they ask.

#3 — They keep dating and treat date night as a sacred ritual.

#2 — When they disagree/argue, their goal is to come to a consensus, not to "win."

#1 — They make daily sacrifices for each other.

Our prayer for your marriage is that you will someday again be able to fulfill the righteous challenge for married couples from Proverbs 5.

> *Drink water from your own cistern, flowing water from your own well. Should your springs be scattered abroad, streams of water in the streets? Let them be for yourself alone, and not for strangers with you. Let your fountain be blessed, and rejoice in the wife of your youth, a lovely deer, a graceful doe. Let her breasts fill you at all times with delight; be intoxicated always in her love* (Proverbs 5:15–19, ESV).

CHAPTER 8
GETTING DISTRACTED

OVERCOMING THE EXHAUSTION OF SADNESS

It has been three years to the day of Adam's death as I write this chapter. Sitting literally in the desert at a friend's house, I reflect and take stock of my wellbeing. In this moment, I realized how my soul resembles my surroundings, dry and barren. I am physically and emotionally exhausted. For three years I have grieved by myself, and grieved with others. For three years I have championed Adam's legacy for the gospel through a foundation we established in honor of him. For three years I have cared for his family, sometimes within my own home and other times waiting for his wife to call and request help. For three years I have tried to help my other children grieve and deal with the challenges of life without Adam. Sitting in the shade to escape the heat of the desert sun, I am forced to admit living in the shadow of grieve is exhausting. Psychologists have identified this exhaustion is the result of the stress of sadness, known as prolonged grief.[19]

Debbie's Journey

My frustration with the question I hear often "why are they still grieving?" is that this question is not thought through! It usually is from someone who hasn't dealt with close personal death or loss or has ignored the whole grief process. Personally, I have felt at times like I am alone in my own grief, this leads me to immediate prayer. This is now what three years looks like for me. Some days I am in a good place reentering activities I used to do and visiting people I haven't seen in a while. I also have been listening to my counselor give me new ways at certain milestones to deal with what she knows is ahead of me. I recently had some solitude time away and focused on the word acceptance. I have come to realize that I have accepted that Adam is with Jesus and that God took him at his appointed time. God designed Adam to leave this earth quickly and with the brain he created.

THE EFFECTS OF THE STRESS OF SADNESS

I fear this chapter may be too technical in its descriptions of the physical and psychological effects of grieving the loss of a loved. However, these detailed descriptions were helpful for me to understand what was happening to my body and mind. The stress of sadness, caused by grief, can lead to many additional physical and men-

[19] American Psychiatric Association, "Prolonged Grief Disorder," https://www.psychiatry.org/patients-families/prolonged-grief-disorder.

tal problems. Prolonged grief, also known as complicated grief, can involve intense pain and emotional distress that persists for months after a loss. People with prolonged grief may have difficulty functioning and may feel detached from others. This emotional distress results in mental and physical maladies associated with chronic stress. "'Young adults who feel down or depressed are more likely to develop cardiovascular disease (CVD) and have poor heart health,' according to a new study led by Johns Hopkins Medicine researchers who analyzed data from more than a half million people between the ages of 18 and 49."[20] The physical impact of the stress of sadness results in higher risks of heart attacks and strokes. "'When you're stressed, anxious or depressed, you may feel overwhelmed, and your heart rate and blood pressure rises. It's also common that feeling down could lead to making poor lifestyle choices like smoking, drinking alcohol, sleeping less and not being physically active—all adverse conditions that negativity impact your heart,' says Garima Sharma, M.B.B.S., associate professor of medicine at Johns Hopkins Medicine, a key author of the study."[21] Other effects of the stress of sadness are feeling overwhelmed, having trouble sleeping, having trouble concentrating, feeling exhausted, having trouble making decisions, and feeling angry, irritable, or easily frustrated.[22]

Long-term sadness has other physiological effects. Stress hormones, that serve a positive purpose to make us more aware when

[20] John Hopkins Medicine, "New study finds-depression poor mental health linked to higher heart disease risks among young adults," (1/30/2023), https://www.hopkinsmedicine.org/news/newsroom/news-releases/2023/01/new-study-finds-depression-poor-mental-health-linked-to-higher-heart-disease-risks-among-young-adults.

[21] Ibid.

[22] Mental Health America, "Stressed or Depressed? Know the Difference," mhanational.org, https://mhanational.org/resources/stressed-or-depressed-know-the-difference/.

we are alone, continue to accumulate after the death of a loved one, creating a constant state of unease. This effect is called "droning" and takes a drastic toll on a person's mental and physical wellbeing.[23] The loneliness signals there is a problem, but it cannot be solved as it would be previously, with contact with the loved one who has passed. The stress of sadness is compounded by the stress of loneliness in prolonged grief. God designed us to be intimate with other people; these connections can be emotional, intellectual, and physical. The relationship that was lost to death had these connections in varying degrees of regularity. To replace that relationship is not simply done and should not be rushed. Instead, the stress of sadness must be responded to in other daily routines and relationships.

I was surprised by the physical symptoms I was having: a racing heart rate, the anxiousness that caused pressure in my chest, even difficulty "catching" my breath. At first, I was not aware of what was happening within my body. As I recognized I was having panic attacks, I knew I had to address the stress of sadness in my life. I have included a box of basic responses to the stress of sadness that I found helpful. This list is not exhaustive nor detailed, but rather meant to give you ideas to pursue in the constant state of unease you are experiencing as you respond to the grief you have endured.

---

[23] Robert Waldinger, M.D. and Marc Schult, Ph.D., "*The Good Life: Lessons From the World's Longest Scientific Study of Happiness*" (Simon and Schuster, 2023), 94.

WAYS TO COPE WITH STRESS AND SADNESS

- Get enough sleep
- Eat a healthy diet
- Exercise regularly
- Focus on the physical world around you (*i.e. say to yourself: "The color of the walls is brown, the carpet is blue, the sky is cloudy"*) as this "grounds" you in reality
- Meditate
- Stay socially connected
- Take medication, if prescribed by a doctor

Note: *The warning signs of Depression will be discussed by mental health experts in chapter 10. If you are dealing with the effects of prolonged sadness you may want to jump ahead to read that chapter.*

TO THOSE RESPONDING TO THE EXHAUSTION OF SADNESS

As the months of grieving kept coming, I was looking for a change in my circumstances. My son was not coming back to me on this side of Heaven, but I knew that my focus needed to change. I was needing a distraction. The grief would still be present, but I needed to find new positive ways to experience life. To prompt my searching for new practices, my counselor asked me what qualities "got me up in the morning?" In other words, what made the day worth living. As I reflected, I realized I needed moments of both curiosity and gratitude to be in my life every day. I also included "play" into my routine. These three qualities set me on new paths of responding to grief. Filling each day with moments of curiosity, gratitude, and play gave me a short-term release of distraction from my grief that enabled me to move forward in dealing with my painful loss by leaps, not mere steps.

I had to become intentional with curiosity, asking new questions about old patterns. I started to research the topic of wellbeing and flourishing as I pictured in my mind what life could be again. I have challenged myself to read a book a month to learn new things about business, leadership, and ministry that I had not considered before. I began to practice new spiritual practices to refresh my daily walking in faith with Jesus. I became disciplined to say quick prayers of gratitude for any small gift from God: a green light on a long drive home, a kind word from a church member, or simply the sight of a butterfly—my sign from God to take a moment and be grateful for this present life, and for Adam, and for what the future would be because of God's goodness.

Play would be harder for me to incorporate into my life. At first, I felt guilty for new joys. However, I saw this too as a gift from God as the Teacher declared, "So I commend the enjoyment of life, because there is nothing better for a person under the sun than to eat and drink and be glad. Then joy will accompany them in their toil all the days of the life God has given them under the sun" (Ecclesiastes 8:15, NIV). I looked forward to the days I get to play with my grandchildren. I found ways to play with my wife at Disneyland, meeting friends and family at the park for fireworks, food, and fun. Play was as simple as walking at the beach, and extreme as exploring a new city in a foreign country.

I don't know what three qualities will become your distractions but ask yourself this question, "What brings you joy?" The Divine Shepherd wants to lead you to new places where you can experience peace and refreshment, "He makes me lie down in green pastures, he leads me beside quiet waters, he refreshes my soul" (Psalm 23:2–3, NIV). God wants to refresh your soul. He wants you to flourish and thrive. Jesus came to restore our lives to the abundance we had in the Garden of Eden (John 10:10). I believe I am on a journey of restoration, and it began by distracting myself from grief with moments of curiosity, gratitude, and play.

Debbie's Journey

This is what I would hope others can fathom before offering their judgments and concerns. Each day looks very different as I live in this shadow. I was just reminded by my granddaughter as she was following her shadow that we can live in this grief and have joy and meaning as we continue to learn to accept what's right in front of us, what God is doing in the present. My prayer life has changed as I look more outward in my grief.

Perhaps before you can identity three qualities to help you get distracted from grief, you need to reduce the stress from the sadness. I have already provided a list of actions you can take but let me discuss in detail how to practice "Mindfulness-Based Stress Reduction."[24] This practice was adapted from Buddhist meditation practices by Jon Kabat-Zinn in 1976. The essential steps are to increase in alertness and attention, being present in the moment to simply observe what is, without passing judgment. I found this process difficult at first, as my mind kept "running off." Being present in the moment was not something I wanted to be. For myself, I started by observing the world around me. Simple observations such as, "the sky is blue" and "the walls are brown." I could not focus on myself yet, so I focused on my surroundings of where I was physically present. The result was the same as the practice was designed to create. I was able to calm my panicked mind. Later I was able to become aware of the sensations my body was experiencing. As I learned to notice my physical surroundings, I have been able to grow in my ability to name my emotions. I can be aware of the stress I am feeling and why I may be feeling it. The goal is not to "name it and fix it," but rather simply to be attentive.

The physical and emotional exhaustion that comes from prolonged grief and the stress of sadness can cause us to live in a sense of autopilot. "Mindfulness-Based Stress Reduction" is meant to do just that, reduce the stress we feel in the moment by focusing on other aspects of our lives. However, sometimes our lives need a "kick start" to focus upon something new. The previously mentioned qualities of curiosity, gratitude and play give me such a distraction to reflect upon. Now let me give you four additional actions that will help create needed distractions as you respond to grief.

---

[24] Ibid., 132.

REVISIT FAVORITE PLACES

Places have memories for us all. The island of Maui contains many memories of my family in happier years. Specific rides at Disneyland, special meals and drinks at restaurants, walks at the harbor are all filled with memories of Adam. You may feel a temptation to avoid visiting these places again in fear of the strong emotions that will come but go anyway! Make visiting these special places sacred. Take time to pause and remember your loved one in that place. Honor your loved one by wearing specific clothing or jewelry. I wear a leather bracelet that I got at Disneyland with Adam's name on it. I wear it daily, most people think it reflects my love of Disneyland, but I know it is a physical reminder of my son.

Every year, our family "retreats" to the desert on the anniversary of Adam's passing. This is a new travel destination for our family as we don't have memories of Adam there. This location is a place to be together and remember Adam. A place of calm and rest. A place to lay in the pool and fall asleep in the desert heat. A place to cry and not draw attention to ourselves. We have found travel to both old and new places to be an important distraction from the grief. Make a list of places that will bring back favorite memories of your loved one and the new places you want to enjoy and expand your memories.

RESTART FAVORITE ACTIVITIES

There is a good chance that when grief interrupted your life, you ceased to do some of your favorite activities. These activities may be simple hobbies you enjoyed or clubs you participated with. If you did these activities with your loved one, it may be very difficult to return to that practice. I know many widows who can no longer attend the same church because it has too many connections to what was experienced as a married couple. Yet, the joy that you experienced in a simple hobby may be just what is needed to distract you from the grief. The time alone in the garden or collecting stamps, will create space to reflect, remember and be aware of what is now happening around you. These activities give life as they renew your joy. One of these activities for me was riding firetrucks as the chaplain for the Orange County Fire Authority in southern California. For a few months after Adam passed, I could not bring myself to a fire station due to the fact I did not want to talk about my son yet. The fire department reached out to us, caring for us with tangible gift cards and many phone calls. So, when I was ready, I visited a crew that I was especially close to and the joy of riding on a fire truck returned to me just like I was 23 again. Today, my role within the fire department is a crucial source of joy and purpose that gives me the needed distraction as I still process my grief.

Organizations that you participated together in previously may be ways to continue the legacy of your loved one in new ways for future generations to experience what your loved one is about. Lean into your "circles" of relationships to find someone who will go with you at first. Allow others to share stories of your loved one as they remember with you who your loved one was. Fill your day with activities that restore life to you, even if it means returning to work. Have a purpose to get up each morning, whether it is to earn money to sustain your family or enjoy an activity that renews you.

REENGAGE WITH FAVORITE PEOPLE

There may be people in your life that you have not had the emotional bandwidth to reengage with until now. Reflect on the messages of condolence you received, note whom you have not connected with in some time. Start small with a simple text back to the person. Consider who you'd like to include in one of your "concentric circles" of trust (see chapter 6 for explanation). The challenge with this step is your "favorite people" may already be those who have been in modes of support for you since the passing of your loved one. The key with these people is to begin to relate to them in new terms, not as those you depend upon for support but now in a mutually reciprocal relationship of giving and receiving love and attention. Go slow with this step as people may interpret this signal of reengagement as meaning you are able to give more than you are ready for. Communicate your boundaries of what you can and cannot give to the person and then stick to these boundaries. Do not feel guilty if some relationships never return to the level of engagement you previously had, you are a new person now and require different relationships.

REINVEST YOURSELF IN NEW INITIATIVES

Lastly, as this is a new season of your life and you are not the same person as before, there may be new activities and initiatives you want to start. For my family, the new initiative was the creation of the Adam Keehn Foundation in honor of our son's passion for the gospel. The Adam Keehn Foundation exists to encourage and inspire young youth pastors to lead students to the gospel of Jesus by providing tangible tools to help a new youth pastor share the gospel of Jesus.[25] We think of "what would the next 'Adam' need to flourish in the beginning of their ministry journey?" Our primary tools we provide are Ministry Development Coaching through personalized mentorship and guidance to help youth pastors grow in their roles and financial grants to assist in their ministry needs. The establishment of this foundation as a 501-c3 nonprofit organization and its development has taken many hours, but it is a blessing to see Adam's legacy continue as we are investing in multiple youth pastors every year, impacting

[25] Please look at our website, AdamKeehnFoundation.com, to understand all we endeavor to do for God's kingdom work and Adam's legacy.

the spiritual journey of thousands of teenagers. This foundation is a distraction. It takes time away from processing my grief; but the grief will be there when the foundation work is done for the day, and I can then reflect both on the loss of Adam and his full impact at the same time because of this new initiative. This does not replace my son but gives me renewed pride in who my son is as I tell his story repeatedly. Be aware this new initiative may result in processing new levels of grief. The emotional toll of telling Adam's story was unexpectedly triggering for new grief experiences. Take note of the new work's impact upon the grieving process and give yourself time to recover. The challenge is not to lose yourself completely in the new initiative as you will still need time to grieve, time to engage with other family members, and time to rest. However, these positive actions make living in the shadow of grief just a little bit more hope-filled as you are expanding your capacity to grieve with hope.

TO THOSE WALKING ALONGSIDE PEOPLE WITH PROLONGED GRIEF

Perhaps the greatest challenge for those who are walking alongside those who are in the depths of prolonged grief, is the sheer amount of time the grieving process is taking. There will be some reasonable "end date" to raw grief, but that conclusion is not up to you. It is not healthy to assume you know better than the person grieving and declare it is time to "move on." If you see unhealthy choices: i.e. substance abuse, bodily neglect, endangerment of dependents, then it is appropriate to seek to intervene. However, grieving is the new normal for the person who has lost a loved one. To stop grieving feels like a betrayal as that is when a person feels truly gone. Instead, patiently help the person change how they grieve.

One way to help change the form of grieving is to ask the person who is grieving to tell you stories about the one who has passed. The remembering and celebrating the accomplishments of the person allows the person to be distracted in the moment. Ask, "how would you want others to remember your loved one?" Is there a memorial or marker that can be established to help people remember and reflect upon this person? It takes a few months for gravestones to be created; this may be a time to hold a special remembrance to honor the person. Tears and emotions will still be a part of the moment, but these distractions help to expand the person's capacity to grieve with hope.

We must remember there is not a timeline for recovering from grief, each person is unique in how they deal with loss. One challenge is you must be patient with those in prolonged grief, as they will have difficulty communicating their emotions and needs. This is especially true with in-laws and others whom they would normally have an intimate relationship with. Instead of pressing for details and connections, we must wait for the grieving person to be ready to receive us. Communicate short messages of love and your presence without expectations. Allow the process to go as long as needed with a focus upon the future, which will be different.

Counseling is an important tool in overcoming prolonged grief. The counseling process may have had "starts and stops" throughout the seasons of grieving, changing counselors and therapies along the way. One therapy to consider is a specialized type of cognitive behavioral therapy (CBT). CBT helps individuals accept the loss and adapt to a world without their loved one while working toward personal goals.[26] One key focus of CBT is to identify and challenge negative

[26] Cleveland Clinic, "Complicated Grief," https://my.clevelandclinic.org/health/diseases/24951-complicated-grief.

thought patterns; this helps the grieving person develop coping skills as they replace the negative talk with a new message of hope. This perspective is based on realistic expectations of life in this new circumstance of doing life without their loved one.

Lastly, as the person begins to live new practices or renewed habits, do not interpret the distraction as the person being "over" grieving the loss of their loved one. The person is simply responding to grief in new expressions. Remember the goal is to change how they express their grief and overcome the exhaustion of sadness. Celebrate the small steps they take with reserved demonstrations of support. These small steps will often be "two steps forward, one step back." What seems to be a "page turned" often is just a momentary distraction from the pain. Support these forms of slow progress, don't allow your frustration to be another burden they must carry.

I understand both perspectives. My grief journey has been different from my wife's, different from my youngest son, and very different from Adam's wife. While I am grieving in a new season with expanded capacities of hope, I too must be patient with the prolonged grief others are facing. I am reminded that not all of Jesus' miracles were done instantaneously. In the gospel of Mark, Jesus led a blind man outside of the city to heal him.

> *When he had spit on the man's eyes and put his hands on him, Jesus asked, "Do you see anything?" He looked up and said, "I see people; they look like trees walking around." Once more Jesus put his hands on the man's eyes. Then his eyes were opened, his sight was restored, and he saw everything clearly* (Mark 8:23–25, NIV).

Why did Jesus' healing of the blind man take a "second application"? Why did not Jesus heal fully the first time? I don't have an answer other than to say, Jesus works uniquely in each of our lives. Our journey with grief may seem similar, but our healing is unique, slow, and in stages. The key is to remember to follow Jesus' lead as the blind man did. To trust the process Jesus is working. Jesus could have spoken for the man's sight to be restored but instead He used spit. As disgusting as this may seem, it was part of the trust the man had to demonstrate. The blind man was willing to allow Jesus to do whatever He thought best. Similarly, as we feel exhausted from the sadness, unable to move beyond deep grieving, we must allow God to shape our understanding and perspectives to see life from His viewpoint. Distractions are one tool that help us move forward to see what could be.

ADAM KEEHN
FOUNDATION

THE ADAM KEEHN FOUNDATION EXISTS TO ENCOURAGE AND INSPIRE YOUNG YOUTH PASTORS TO LEAD STUDENTS TO THE GOSPEL OF JESUS

WE FUND TANGIBLE TOOLS TO HELP A NEW YOUTH PASTOR SHARE THE GOSPEL OF JESUS... TOOLS FOR THE "NEXT ADAM"!

@adamkeehnfoundation

@adamkeehnfoundation

adamkeehnfoundation.com

adamkeehnfoundation@gmail.com

SECTION 3

LIVING WITH GRIEF

Eventually the grieving changes. The rawness of emotions ebbs away. The suffocation of pain and stress ease a bit, and you will find yourself living in a new, unwanted, "normal." What remains however, is the gaping hole in your life. A black hole that sucks all aspects of life into its vortex and does not let go. This section is about aspects that resemble living in this new reality. This next stage of grieving may still involve deep emotional pain and depressive modes as we adjust to new expectations of our core relationships.

CHAPTER 9

LIVING WITH A BROKEN HEART

Debbie's Journey

It's painful for me, accepting the lives that will never be what I dreamed and hoped for, dreams not coming to fruition here on this side of Heaven. I am still struggling with accepting how lives have changed because of this. In writing this, I have decided to keep my family's privacy and not name them. I sit and watch a little girl who will not know her Dad, and all his beautiful characteristics. His beautiful wife who sees him every day in their daughter and doesn't have him there to share in parenting and marriage. I listen to his sister and how her hurt of the two of them not having the families together to grow with one another and celebrate the growth of their children. Not hearing enough of Uncle Adam in her household and vice versa. His brother who is just beginning to enter adulthood and needs his older brother there for him, how is this shaping him now. This is just a glimpse! It's living with a broken heart.

This has been one of the hardest chapters to write in this book as I must confront the fact that my heart is still broken for the loss of my son. Using the iceberg analogy, people only see the man I display. A man who can smile and enjoy the day God has given him. A man who seems to have "moved on" in some aspects of life. Those perceptions are true. I am able to experience the peace and joy of God, but "under the water line," I am still aching for my son and what would have been.

I miss most watching Adam in ministry, sharing the gospel of Jesus as a young youth pastor. I miss playing with him and his daughter, celebrating my grandparenting years as they "should have been." The pain of mourning "what will never be" is a pain that I suffer alone as no one else, not even me, knew what could have been. The pain of losing "what was" has deep and beautiful memories to hold onto. The pain of losing Adam as a young man who was married and passionate for Jesus is something that I can celebrate over and over again, bringing smiles to my face. But my heart is broken when trying to overcome a pain that I cannot even put a picture to memory or an experience to be an anchor in time.

I am not sure how to live with a broken heart. I think this is the "shadow" of grief that continually follows me. I do not have many tools to offer in this ongoing situation, except to bend your perspective to what Paul had to surrender to. Paul lived with ongoing pain. Paul pleaded for the pain to be taken away. God, however, did not take away Paul's pain, but instead gave him the strength through grace to continue in his journey. In Paul's second epistle to the Corinthian church, he reflected on this pain. "Therefore, in order to keep me from becoming conceited, I was given a thorn in my flesh, a messenger of Satan, to torment me. Three times I pleaded with the Lord to take it away from me" (2 Corinthians 12:7b–8, NIV). There has been great debate on what the "thorn" was. David Guzik cites different early church traditions offering ideas on what this ongoing pain was. "Tertullian gives the earliest recorded guess at the exact nature of Paul's problem. He thought the thorn in the flesh was an earache or a headache… historian Sir William Ramsay offered the suggestion that Paul's infirmity was a type of malaria common to the area where he served as a missionary."[27] By looking at the original language Paul wrote in, we know from the words Paul chose to describe his suffering, that the pain was intense, even violent against him. Paul used the word *thorn*, which has the root word used to describe a tent stake, not a thumbtack.[28] Secondly, we know that this thorn was "given to" torment Paul, implying this thorn was experienced as "to strike with a fist, treat with violence." From the grammar, the last important observation is this was done to Paul, allowed by God. The passive voice makes it clear Paul did not do anything to deserve this; he was not active in producing its outcomes. The Scriptures tell us the thorn was ultimately given by God, but it was also a messenger of Satan. This reminds us of the story of Job, where God allowed Satan to inflict suffering upon Job. In both cases, Job's and Paul's, divine wisdom determined that the hardship, i.e. thorn, was needed. To summarize, we know this issue was a major source of pain and frustration that Paul pleaded for God to remove, as it was a pain he did not deserve. The

---

[27] David Guzik, "Study Guide for 2 Corinthians 12," https://www.blueletterbible.org/comm/guzik_david/study-guide/2-corinthians/2-corinthians-12.cfm?a=1090001.

[28] Strong's Lexicon, "G4647 – *skolops*." https://www.blueletterbible.org/lexicon/g4647/kjv/tr/0-1/.

idea Paul prayed three times is a Hebrew figure of speech that really means much more than three times, it's a continual cry.[29] Paul was living with ongoing pain and continuously prayed for relief. I know that feeling. There are moments I simply want to tear off my skin and scream. The pain of not having what was meant to be, at least in my mind, is crippling at times as I think of my granddaughter growing up without her father to guide her. The pain of a broken heart seems to be a constant simmer of grief that demands to be acknowledge. God's response to Paul is exactly what I must focus upon each day as I live with a broken heart.

Paul had to surrender to the grace of God. God's response to Paul is the often-quoted verse that is difficult to truly understand. "But he said to me, 'My grace is sufficient for you, for my power is made perfect in weakness.' Therefore I will boast all the more gladly about my weaknesses, so that Christ's power may rest on me" (2 Corinthians 12:9, NIV). Grace is the true goodness of God we don't deserve but are given anyway. What God gave Paul was the goodness of God that would be enough. Enough. Sufficient. This calls for faithful surrender to God, as what I deem "enough" may be different from what God intends to give. David Guzik in his study guide on 2 Corinthians said,

> *Paul was desperate in his desire to find relief from this burden, but there are two ways of relief. It can come by removing the load or by strengthening the shoulder that bears the load. Instead of taking away the thorn, God strengthened Paul under it, and God would show His strength through Paul's apparent weakness.* [30]

---

[29] G. Campbell Morgan, *The Corinthian Letters of Paul* (Fleming H. Revell, 1946), 267.

[30] David Guzik, "Study Guide for 2 Corinthians 12."

When we are going through difficult times it is hard to accept that God will sustain us, that Jesus is enough to help me bear the burden. This is the battle of faith, to believe God knows my situation and still allowed me to experience the pain and suffering and that only what He can give me is enough to get me through this moment, and the next… and the next.

This grace is a gift of goodness that empowered Paul in hardships. God's grace, the goodness of Christ, gives us God's power. There is false thinking in our world, and it is often said at moments of crisis, pain, or loss; it is the myth "God never gives us more than we can handle." While aspects of this statement are true, as God won't let you be tempted to sin where you can't resist (1 Corinthians 10:13) but that's not the intent of that saying. That saying is false thinking because the focus is on us, what we can handle. Apart from God's grace, I cannot handle this ongoing pain of a broken heart. The strength of God, the power of God is the focus of God's assertion, and we must get out of God's way by surrendering to the grace of God.

As troubling as it may be to think about this, God intentionally gave Paul debilitating pain of some kind so he would be in constant, total dependence on God's strength, this is the grace of God. It is difficult for my mind to understand, that I will best understand God's goodness in my utter weakness and pain. However, this dependence upon God is the key response for living with a broken heart. We must surrender to God's purpose and grace to live in that reality. However, this is so much easier to say and write, than to live. Surrendering to God is often misunderstood and underestimated. We sing of it easily, yet when the circumstances of life challenge us, we rise to fight for our needs, for our comfort. Surrender is dropping all your needs, this includes our physical, emotional, and spiritual needs. Dropping your need for comfort or relief from the pain. We surrender because we know, i.e. we accept, that everything that happens, all that comes our way, has happened by God's will and by God's permission. Pause, read that again, let that truth sink in. Proverbs 3:5–6 assures us "Trust in the LORD with all your heart and lean not on your own understanding; in all your ways submit to him, and he will direct your paths" (NIV). God will strengthen us to walk in the pain as He directs us to His purposes. Surrender is practiced by continually losing your own will in the will of God. You desire only what He desires, that is what He has desired for all eternity

Jeane Guyon wrote the reflection, *Experiencing the Depths of God*, in 1685, over 300 years ago. She used the older English word *abandonment* for our idea of surrender; however, that's a powerful way of thinking of what it means to surrender to the grace of God: we abandon our needs and demands.[31] We are able to do this as we become content with the current moment, regardless of its contents, knowing that God's eternal plan for you is present in every moment. That is abandonment, entrusting the future to Him, and giving your entire present to your Lord. This was the posture Paul took in his surrendering of his circumstances to the grace of God.

Paul determined in verse 9 that he would focus his attention on this grace of God and not the continuing pain that was allowed to remain. The result was "Christ's power may rest on me," which can be literally translated, that Christ may "pitch his tent" with me. What a beautiful image of being fathered by God. To have God's love, grace, and power surround me, envelope me as one may lay in a tent, being strengthened to finish the journey—no matter how difficult it may be. I picture a dad running beside a young son learning to ride a bike, holding on the boy's shoulder, steadying him in his wobbles so he does not fall off. Or a dad coming to a teenage son with firm but

---

[31] Jeanne Guyon, *Experiencing the Depths of Jesus Christ* (Seed Sowers Publishing, 1981), 35.

loving words, giving guidance in tough choices to help make him the man he is meant to become. We have a loving heavenly Father who gave Paul exactly what he needed, a thorn in the flesh, and gave him the strength to continue by the grace and the power of God. This is what living with a broken heart means. To affix your focus on God so you are strengthened to live with the pain of what will never be in the grief, as you receive the goodness of God, which is enough. The ongoing living with a broken heart is remedied in surrender to God. This is not a passive endurance but actively yielding to God's purpose.

Paul's summary of his journey with pain and hardship declares, "That is why, for Christ's sake, I delight in weaknesses, in insults, in hardships, in persecutions, in difficulties. For when I am weak, then I am strong" (2 Corinthians 12:10, NIV). I am not at the point where I delight in my loss or pain, but I am realizing that when I am weak, then I am strong because of what God alone gives me. Paul came to this same conclusion that through surrender to God, accepting the burdens of suffering, he then received the power of God—strength to continue!

TO THOSE LIVING WITH A "HEART-CONDITION"

I have struggled to understand how I am to continue living with my broken heart in daily practical terms. After much reflection I decided that the best way forward is to describe how we live in such surrender to God as responses to a medical heart condition. The applications prescribed by a doctor will be our metaphor.[32]

CHANGES ARE NEEDED TO BE MADE

Doctors will begin their instructions to patients with heart conditions discussing the lifestyle changes that need to be made—bad habits that must be stopped, daily exercise and nutrition changes to start. It may be that your lifestyle took a turn for the worse as you grieved the loss of your loved one. I had very little energy to do very much, except sit still and ponder. We developed the routine of walking in some of Adam's favorite spots along the beach and harbor. However, those were more for talking and remembering together, not exercise. As Debbie and I grieved, we would go through seasons where we would "eat our feelings." Calming our frayed nerves and spinning minds with tubs of Thrifty's ice cream. I do mean tubs. One for Debbie. One for me. We ate our grief to the point when I went into the doctor's office for my annual physical, he was alarmed that my sugar levels had become pre-diabetic. A change was needed.[33]

Debbie and I had to identity the bad habits that we had allowed to become a mode of operation. Some of you may have turned to substances, alcohol, or other drugs, to numb the pain. These vices will only momentarily relieve the pain you are living with. If the abuse

[32] Please give me grace in using this analogy as I know that for those of you living with a real medical heart condition must take this very seriously and I do not mean to make light of that condition. My daughter was a nurse in the ICU Heart Institute at the Children's Hospital of Los Angeles for 4 years and I heard her first-hand accounts of the pain and sorrow parents had to endure watching their child suffer with a medical heart condition. I share this information to assure you I use this analogy simply as a process to move forward with an emotionally broken heart.

[33] I am pleased to report and calm your fears for me that I have changed my eating patterns and have greatly reduced my glucose (sugar) levels and am no longer pre-diabetic!

of these substances has become an issue, recognized in the fact you cannot function daily without them, you need to seek help. Recovery groups or professional therapy may be a necessary inclusion to your new routine to change the bad habits.

I have often found it is easier to stop a bad habit by starting new good habits. For Debbie and I this was a refocus on daily exercise. We committed to walking a strenuous two-and-a-half-mile path at the beach daily. We changed our diet to greatly limit sugar in our meals. We have replaced the ice cream with healthier snacks or cheeses. The resulting physical feeling by including exercise and healthy nutrition has created new sources of energy to combat the negative feelings grief brings. There is a direct connection between physical health and your emotional health. When your body is feeling "right," then your head and heart have an easier time focusing their energy on healing the pain of loss. There is also a synergetic connection between your physical health and your spiritual wellbeing. The better shape your physical body is in, the greater the impact various spiritual disciplines will have in your life, and vice versa. Prayer, solitude, and fasting have been spiritual practices that I have added to my faith routines. Morning Scripture reading, especially reading and praying the psalms, has sustained me from the moment Adam passed away; however, these new practices have enriched my spiritual life, benefitting my physical and emotional conditions.

OTHER INTERVENTIONS

Doctors may also prescribe medication to help control specific dangers of a medical heart condition, such as high blood pressure. These medicine dosages must be strictly followed. In the same way, there have been seasons in my living in the shadow of grief that I have taken a low dosage of an anti-anxiety medication to help me focus and calm my "racing" mind. The wave of panic that my mind would encounter caused my heart to be overwhelmed in the moment, unable to function. Twice I have gone to the emergency room thinking I was having a heart attack, only to discover it was simply my emotions causing me to panic. I have taken these medications, sought counseling to alleviate the panic by understanding its source, and learned breathing techniques to ward off the feelings of panic when I notice their appearance. I have recently weaned myself off these medications as the sense of crisis and panic has eased. I vulnerably share my journey to let you know that God has used many different tools in my life to help me overcome the impact of grief. He has used His Word, times of prayer and other spiritual practices; but God has also used therapists and medicine to bring His peace into my life at moments of pain and panic.

You must follow what you believe is helpful and good, regardless of what other people say about it. I have not resorted to extreme natural drugs or practices (i.e. hallucinogenic mushrooms, ayahuasca) in my recovery from deep grief. Some friends have encouraged me to try these homeopathic remedies, citing the benefits they have experienced from its consumption. You must find a path forward that follows your moral and religious beliefs that yields the relief you are needing.

Lastly, doctors will instruct you to manage your stress triggers. We have already discussed dealing with the stress of grief in a previous chapter, so we will simply encourage you to reread chapter 8. However, it was interesting in my research into doctors' advice for dealing with heart conditions the emphasis on seeking emotional support from other people, especially a licensed therapist if needed, was highlighted in the research. We have discussed the need for circles of support from your community in chapter 6, and it is reassuring to know this also follows the best medical advice available. God created our bodies to be lived in community and medical science affirms this view of creation. While this has been a brief overview of medical responses to living with a heart condition, the applications of this analogy are well-heeded in dealing with an emotionally broken heart.

By thinking of living with a broken heart as a serious emotional condition that requires the diligence of responding to a serious medical condition, you will find the motivation to do the hard work that encourages healthy growth: physically, emotionally, and spiritually. The apostle Paul used the running of a race as a metaphor for the discipline and endurance required to compete for the prize.

> *Do you not know that in a race all the runners run, but only one gets the prize? Run in such a way as to get the prize. Everyone who competes in the games goes into strict training. They do it to get a crown that will not last, but we do it to get a crown that will last forever. Therefore I do not run like someone running aimlessly; I do not fight like a boxer beating the air. No, I strike a blow to my body and make it my slave so that after I have preached to others, I myself will not be disqualified for the prize* (1 Corinthians 9:24–27, NIV).

May you run with this broken heart, knowing that God will give you a blessing that will last forever.

WALKING ALONGSIDE SOMEONE WITH A BROKEN HEART

Remember the person who is grieving and living with a broken heart is overwhelmed with a continuous flood of emotions and stressors. Please make sure not to add to their burden by commenting what you think they should be doing or feeling by now. I can tell you from experience, this person does not want to feel the ongoing pain and loss of their loved one. They too want to escape this moment, but they will not be able to on this side of Heaven. That's their reality. Therefore, you must continue to practice the previous steps of waiting and praying. However, let me highlight three practices you can do now to help this person living with a broken heart.

ADVOCATE AND LISTEN

Just as a medical patient may need others to advocate for appropriate treatment, the same is true for those living with a broken heart. There may be times to speak up to those around the person grieving, to promote healthy barriers and loving words. The extended grieving period, that most will not understand, can cause some people—with good intentions but harmful responses—to seek to "push" a person out of grieving and onto "normal" living. These are the moments an advocate is needed. An advocate has the other person's best interest in focus, even if it is time-consuming and uncomfortable to stand in this position. An advocate has a long-term perspective. They must keep this patient approach to make sure to provide the grieving heart what is needed in this moment.

Listening is also what a caregiver can give. Listening to a grieving person spew painful thoughts. These are difficult to listen to without trying to correct, but it is a listening posture that allows the person who has lost such a massive part of their life to digest this new reality by verbally wrestling with what is, and it is not what is wanted. We have discussed being present and listening previously in this book so we will not belabor the point except to highlight the importance of continuously being present in a listening posture for whenever the brokenness needs to be shared. One last thought on listening, make sure to listen for non-verbal cues to identify what the true message is that is being spoken.

PROMOTE PHYSICAL ACTIVITY AND HEALTHY NUTRITION

When you are tempted to speak, promote healthy alternatives. For Debbie and me, when we recognized our need to change our practice of "eating our grief" through tubs of ice cream, we were ready to listen to the nutritional ideas of others. We often said "yes" to people's invitations to take a walk. Friends took us out to dinner at "healthier" restaurants and modeled not drinking alcohol or soda at the meal, only water. What we found helpful was the example set for us in an invitational, non-preachy, manner. We heard their message from the actions displayed before us. This "come do with us" not "go do yourself" approach was the welcoming gesture that Debbie and I could take, or leave, as we were ready. One simple place to start is to find out which physical activities they enjoy best and joining them.

KNOW HOW TO MONITOR SYMPTOMS

In the next chapter we will discuss the symptoms of clinical depression to be aware of dangerous patterns in the grieving person's behavior. As it is important to learn the danger signs of a worsening medical heart condition (i.e. shortness of breath, fatigue, leg swelling, and feeling light-headed), so too when grief is turning into chronic depression it will give warning signs. Depression involves a persistent low mood and loss of interest for an extended period, and often includes feelings of worthlessness and suicidal thoughts, which are less common in grief. Thoughts of death in grief may be related to wanting to be with the deceased. In depression, thoughts of death can be focused on ending one's life due to feelings of hopelessness or an inability to cope with the pain of depression. Please make sure to read the next chapter that was written by a licensed clinical therapist to understand these warning signs to look for.

REMEMBER TO LOOK AFTER YOURSELF

Lastly, remember you too are hurting. You are grieving the loss of the person. You must make sure not to lose yourself in the grief of someone else. In many ways, you may become the caregiver of the person dealing with a broken heart. You may need to find breaks in the daily routine of being with the person grieving. The benefit of a ten-minute walk outside can be refreshing, not just in the air you breathe, but also the perspective that creation gives us. Take time to do something you love. You may also need to socialize with other people, staying connected to other people in different spheres of life. The caregiving of someone with a broken heart needs to be a "community effort" in that it will take more than one person to become the support system required in living in the shadow of grief.

CHAPTER 10 DIFFERENT FROM GRIEF: *IS IT DEPRESSION?*

By Laura Wingard, MA, MS, LMFT

LET ME INTRODUCE LAURA

We adopted our son Mfundo from South Africa when he was two years old. When our son was in the third grade, he began to display troubling behaviors that needed some intervention. Debbie and I found Laura through a trusted friend's recommendation, and she has partnered with our family through numerous seasons of challenging growth. Laura has always provided wise and caring advice to us, and when Adam passed away, she was part of the care team we assembled for our family. As we were brainstorming what elements would make this book most helpful to people who are in a season of grieving or walking alongside someone who has lost a loved one, we thought of Laura and asked her to write this chapter on explaining depression and how it is different from grief. She will also present the warning signs of depression to look for and to know when intervention is warranted. I am thankful for Laura's willingness to write this chapter based her years of training and experience as a licensed therapist. Please heed her words that follow...

The words grief and depression are often spoken in the same sentence because they can both involve deep pain and a profound sense of loss. Yet while they may look similar on the surface, they are fundamentally different experiences, especially from a mental health standpoint. As a therapist, I have sat with many individuals navigating the complicated terrain of grief and others weighed down by the clinical burden of depression. Each experience is real, valid, and deeply personal—but confusing the two can lead to missed opportunities for support, misunderstood pain, spiritual growth and even misdiagnosis.

This chapter explores the nuanced distinctions between grief and depression, helping readers understand how to identify each, how they overlap, and why knowing the difference matters. Drawing from years as a youth pastor, clinician and of practicing therapy, I aim to illuminate how mental health professionals assess, support, and walk alongside those who are grieving, as well as those who are experiencing depression—and sometimes, those navigating both at once.

Grief and Depression: Clinical Insight

While grief and depression can appear strikingly similar—both marked by intense sadness, disrupted sleep, fatigue, and changes in weight and appetite—their underlying causes, emotional experiences, and paths to healing are fundamentally different. Grief is typically a natural response to loss, such as the death of a loved one, the end of a meaningful relationship or dream job, and it often comes in waves, interspersed with moments of relief or even positive memories. Depression, by contrast, tends to be more *pervasive and persistent*, often emerging without a clear external trigger and characterized by a profound sense of hopelessness, worthlessness, and a loss of interest or pleasure in previously enjoyed activities.[34] In terms of treatment, grief may resolve over time with emotional support and personal reflection, whereas clinical depression often requires professional intervention, including therapy, medication, or both. Understanding these differences is essential for providing the appropriate support and care to those who are suffering.

Adaptive Grief

Adaptive Grief[35] is a *non-pathological response*[36] to loss—a natural and often sacred experience that occurs when something or someone deeply meaningful is no longer present. It is the heart's way of honoring love, attachment, and the significance of what has been lost. Far from being an illness, grief is understood clinically as a normal and necessary process of adaptation, allowing individuals to integrate loss into their lives over time. Grief

---

[34] Major Depressive Disorder criteria are adapted from the *Diagnostic and statistical manual of mental disorders* (5th ed., text rev.; DSM-5-TR; American Psychiatric Association, 2022).

[35] Adaptive (or "normal") grief refers to the natural bereavement process in which individuals gradually adjust to loss, integrate it into their lives, and continue to function without meeting criteria for a mental disorder (American Psychiatric Association, 2022). *Diagnostic and statistical manual of mental disorders.*

[36] In clinical contexts, "non-pathological" describes experiences or responses that are within the range of normal human functioning and not reflective of a mental disorder. J. C. Wakefield, "The concept of mental disorder: On the boundary between biological facts and social values," *American Psychologist, 47*(3), (1992): 373–388.

does not follow a single predictable path; it may ebb and flow, sometimes quiet and subtle, other times overwhelming and consuming. It can surface in emotional, physical, cognitive, behavioral, or even spiritual forms. While the death of a loved one is perhaps the most recognized source of grief, it can also emerge after divorce, miscarriage, the loss of a job, the diagnosis of illness, displacement, or other life transitions. Each expression of grief is unique, shaped by culture, personality, faith, relationships, and circumstance, but at its core, grief reflects the universal human capacity to love, and the profound ache of having to let go. Below are some of the common key elements of grief.

Key Clinical Characteristics of Grief[37]

- **Waves of emotion:** Intense sadness comes in waves, often triggered by reminders of the loss, and can alternate with moments of peace or even joy.
- **Preserved self-esteem:** Individuals in grief usually maintain a sense of self-worth, even amidst sadness.
- **Focus on the loss:** Thoughts tend to center on the deceased or the lost relationship, rather than a pervasive negative view of self, world, or future.
- **Gradual integration:** Over time, the intensity of grief typically lessens, and the person begins to re-engage with life, though they may continue to feel moments of sadness indefinitely.

---

[37] Grief is defined as the emotional response to the loss of someone or something significant, encompassing psychological, behavioral, social, and physical reactions (American Psychiatric Association, 2022). *Diagnostic and statistical manual of mental disorders.*

A very common model of grief is encompassed in *The Cycle of Grief*, often referred to as the Five Stages of Grief.[38] This cycle was introduced by Elisabeth Kübler-Ross in her 1969 book *On Death and Dying* (as Dave has referenced in an earlier chapter). Originally, this model was developed to describe the emotional journey of terminally ill patients facing their own death, but it has since been widely applied to anyone experiencing loss.

The Five Stages of Grief (Kübler-Ross Model)

- **Denial**—Refusing to accept the reality of the loss; a defense mechanism to buffer the initial shock and inability to process what is happening, especially if it is sudden loss. This is a common first response but not always. Some people may skip denial entirely and immediately feel cycles of anger and blame. The person struggles to accept the loss, feeling numb or in disbelief. *"This can't be real. The doctors must be wrong—they'll walk through the door any moment."*
- **Anger**—Feelings of frustration and helplessness may be directed at others, oneself, or even loved ones who have died. Emotions commonly come out as frustration, resentment, or irritability. *"Why did this have to happen? It's not fair! The Drs should have done more to prevent this."*
- **Bargaining**—Attempting to negotiate or make deals with God or others in hopes of reversing or lessening the loss. *"If I just do everything right, maybe things will get better. Please, if I pray hard enough, can I have them back?"*

[38] Elizabeth Kübler-Ross, *On Death and Dying: What the Dying Have to Teach Doctors, Nurses, Clergy and Their Own Families* (Macmillan, 1969).

- **Depression** — Deep sadness, withdrawal, hopelessness, and emotional pain as the reality of the loss sets in. *"They're really gone... I don't know how I can keep going without them."*
- **Acceptance** — The loss is acknowledged, and the person begins to adapt and move forward, carrying the memory with them. A true coming to terms with the loss and beginning to move forward, even though the pain may still exist. *"I'll always miss them, but I can find a way to keep living and honor their memory."*

A dangerous misconception of the *Cycle of Grief* is that it is linear. The stages are *not linear*—people may cycle between these stages or experience them in a different order or not experience certain stages at all. Though denial is a common first stage it is not the first stage for all who are grieving. Just as acceptance isn't the final stage in the sense that a person may accept certain parts of their grief but still experience denial, anger about other parts of their grief even after they have accepted the loss. Kübler-Ross later clarified that the model was not meant to be prescriptive, but rather a framework to help understand common grief responses. For many clinicians, these stages are a gross oversimplification of grief and can cause guilt for many people who don't feel they ever stop grieving. The loss is always there; it may change but there really is no end for grief. Many just learn how to live with and cope better with grief over time.

I recently lost my stepdad to a long battle with Alzheimer's disease. Even as I write, I realize he left us three years ago but, for me, some parts of my grief still feel so present and raw. When you lose a parent, it can feel like layers of never-ending loss and some days the grief can feel entirely too heavy. Just the other day, I was driving with my four-year-old son and the song "Cheeseburger In Paradise" by Jimmy Buffett came on my Spotify. My stepdad was a big fan and our family was commonly spotted at a Jimmy concert singing along. At first, I was driving and singing happily with my son but then the grief hit hard. My eyes filled with tears and I wished so desperately that my stepdad would be here to see my son grow into a man. The grief struck deeply in such an unpredictably random way that day. Music is a common trigger for me. I then quickly got angry (back to the second stage of grief in an instant), I was so mad that my son wouldn't have his Papa's love and joy, he wouldn't be there to see him graduate kindergarten or take him on his first trip to Catalina Island (blasting Jimmy Buffett of course). I cried the whole way home just because of a silly Jimmy Buffett song. The depression stage sat with me all day.

Depressive Disorders

In contrast to grief, depression is a mental illness which affects *all* aspects of daily functioning: work, sleeping, eating, school, hobbies, relationships, motivation, etc., and commonly has more concerning and sometimes life-threatening symptoms.[39] It is important to know the specific symptoms of depression and how they may look different from grief because early intervention is hugely important for successful depression treatment planning. In the very least, if there is any question, know the need to consult with a professional as soon as possible for assessment. If people, especially those in caretaking professions[40] have even minimal psychoeducation on the symptoms of depression, then these symptoms can be caught and treated as early as possible.

---

[39] American Psychiatric Association. (2022). *Diagnostic and statistical manual of mental disorders.*

[40] In psychology, "caretaking positions" often refer to relational roles in which an individual assumes responsibility for another's emotional or physical well-being, sometimes at the expense of their own needs. (Cermak, 1986; Hooper, 2007). Cermak, T. L. (1986). *Diagnosing and treating co-dependence: A guide for professionals who work with chemical dependents, their spouses, and children.* Johnson Institute Books.

Clinical depression is a highly treatable disorder, and with swift early intervention, depression can quickly be stabilized through psychotherapy and medication[41] (only when necessary). An important skill is for most people to be able to differentiate between an adaptive grief period and the early signs of depression as it can help assure proper care. As reported by National Institute on Mental Health (NIH), "an estimated 21.0 million adults in the United States had at least one major depressive episode. This number represented 8.3% of all U.S. adults."[42] This number is even higher for adolescents, NIH reports, "in 2021, an estimated 3.7 million adolescents aged 12 to 17 in the United States had at least one major depressive episode with severe impairment in the past year. This number represented 14.7% of the U.S. population aged 12 to 17."[43]

The most concerning difference between grief and depression is the increase in threat of suicidal ideation with severe forms of depression. A constant concern when treating depression is the possible presence suicidal ideation: thinking about, considering, or planning suicide. It is very common for clinically depressed individuals to experience extreme feelings of despair, loneliness, and hopelessness that may lead to thoughts of suicide. When depression begins to feel increasingly more despair-

---

[41] Common medications for Major Depressive Disorder include selective serotonin reuptake inhibitors (SSRIs) such as fluoxetine, sertraline, and citalopram; serotonin-norepinephrine reuptake inhibitors (SNRIs) such as venlafaxine and duloxetine; atypical antidepressants such as bupropion and mirtazapine; tricyclic antidepressants (TCAs) such as amitriptyline; and monoamine oxidase inhibitors (MAOIs) such as phenelzine. Choice of medication depends on symptom profile, side effect tolerance, and patient history.

[42] National Institute of Mental Health, "Mental Health Information: Statistics – Major Depression" (retrieved Nov. 15, 2025). https://www.nimh.nih.gov/health/statistics/major-depression.

[43] Ibid.

ing, with no perceived way out, death may feel like the only viable escape from overwhelming sadness. Suicidal thoughts are often more about ending the emotional pain rather than desiring actual death. Death, therefore, seems like the only way to end the pain. Some people may have thoughts of suicide but have no actual intent to end their lives. Suicidal thoughts are much different from an actual plan to complete suicide. For other people, though, thoughts of suicide are accompanied with intent and a plan to complete suicide.

Although suicidality is not always present with symptoms of major depression, it is important to remember that suicidal individuals are almost always struggling with some form of depression, and that assessing suicidal intent can be complex and difficult. If more people know the distinct difference between grief and depression, then those suffering with depression can also receive proper care and ongoing suicide assessment from a caring professional.

According to NIH, in 2023 "suicide was the eleventh leading cause of death overall in the United States, claiming the lives of over 49,300 people. Suicide was the second leading cause of death among individuals between the ages of 10 and 34 and the fourth leading cause of death among individuals between the ages of 35 and 44. There were over two times as many suicides (49,316) in the United States as there were homicides (22,830)."[44]

Suicidal ideation is a serious mental health concern that is highly linked to depression rather than to adaptive grief. While grief is a natural and temporary response to loss, depression can create pervasive feelings of hopelessness, distorted thinking, and an increased risk of self-harm. This distinction underscores

[44] National Institute of Mental Health, "Statistics – suicide," https://www.nimh.nih.gov/health/statistics/suicide (retrieved Nov. 15, 2025).

the importance of accurate assessment, as misattributing suicidal thoughts to grief rather than underlying depressive symptoms can delay critical intervention. Effective treatment—whether therapy, medication, or supportive care—targets depression, not grief alone, helping individuals regain hope, stabilize mood, and reduce the risk of suicide.

Types of Depression[45]

Major Depressive Disorder (MDD)

- Sad feelings most of the day, nearly every day for at least two consecutive weeks
- Experience a loss of interest or pleasure in activities (such as socializing, sports, hobbies) that were once meaningful to them
- Weight gain or loss
- Fatigue, sleep disturbances
- Feelings of worthlessness, difficulty concentrating
- Thoughts of death

Persistent Depressive Disorder (PDD)

- Typically feel depressed most of the day, for more days than not, for at least two years

[45] The DSM-5-TR recognizes several depressive disorders, including Major Depressive Disorder, Persistent Depressive Disorder (Dysthymia), Disruptive Mood Dysregulation Disorder, Premenstrual Dysphoric Disorder, Substance/Medication-Induced Depressive Disorder, and Depressive Disorder Due to Another Medical Condition (American Psychiatric Association, 2022). American Psychiatric Association. (2022). *Diagnostic and statistical manual of mental disorders.*

- PDD includes most symptoms seen in MDD, with the notable exception of suicidal thoughts and feelings
- Those with PDD may experience relief from their symptoms for up to two months at a time

Persistent Grief Disorder (PGD)

- Intense, persistent yearning or preoccupation with the deceased, difficulty accepting the death, identity disruption, and feelings of emptiness or meaninglessness
- Duration: Symptoms persist 12+ months in adults (6+ months in children/adolescents), exceeding the expected cultural norms of mourning
- Impact: Grief remains chronic and disabling, interfering with daily functioning, relationships, and ability to adapt to life after the loss

Deeper Look Into the Symptoms of Depression (MDD)

Clinical depression or MDD is a diagnosable mental health condition that affects mood, cognition, behavior, and physical health. It is not necessarily tied to a specific loss or event, and it can emerge spontaneously. Common things to look for with MDD:

- **Pervasive low mood:** Sadness or emptiness is present most of the day, nearly every day, often without external triggers
- **Anhedonia:** A marked loss of interest or pleasure in almost all activities
- **Negative self-concept:** Feelings of worthlessness, excessive guilt, or self-blame are common

- **Cognitive distortion:** Thoughts may become hopeless, pessimistic, and even suicidal
- **Functional impairment:** Daily functioning—at work, in relationships, or in self-care—is often significantly impaired
- **Duration and severity:** Symptoms persist for at least two weeks, but often much longer if untreated
- **Physical symptoms:** low energy, fatigue, sleep disturbances (insomnia and/or hypersomnia), increased or decreased appetite, headaches, chronic pain
- **Psychological symptoms:** Aggression, agitation, difficulty making decisions, poor concentration, low self-esteem, hopelessness, guilt, self-reproach, loneliness, feeling empty, feelings of despair, feelings of worthlessness, concurrent anxiety
- **Social symptoms:** Isolation from others, avoidance of others, lack of motivation to move toward others, lack of engagement in activities with others, difficulty engaging in pleasurable experiences, feeling unable to relate to others.
- **Spiritual concerns:** Lack of meaning and purpose, insecurity and self-doubt, guilt and shame, feelings of worthlessness relative to God, doubt, apathy

What Depression Can Look Like:

- Marked changes in sleep patterns
- Lack of proper hygiene (consider what is normal for the person's age and income level)
- Withdrawal and isolating behavior (for example, avoiding conversation)
- Decrease in normal activities (doesn't show up for social events or other functions)
- Difficulty going to work or school

- Making comments such as "I don't feel myself lately" or "I feel empty inside"
- Expressing sadness for no identifiable reason
- Difficulty paying attention

For those of us in caretaking roles, you may need to do initial assessment to decide next steps. According to the National Alliance on Mental Health,[46] the following questions are appropriate to ask yourself or someone (family, friends, teachers, etc.) when assessing for possible a depressive disorder:

* Do you constantly feel sad or empty, like you feel nothing at all?
- Do you feel like everything is going wrong?
- Do you feel worthless? Guilty?
- Are you irritable most of the time?
* Do you spend a lot of time isolated from friends and family?
- Do you still enjoy hobbies you used to enjoy?
- Are you sleeping more? Sleeping less?
- Have your eating habits changed?
- Do you have normal levels of energy?
* Do you ever think about dying? Have you ever tried to harm yourself?

---

[46] Joyce Burland, *NAMI Family-to-Family: Class 2 Participant Manual* (2020), 41–42. https://namiwestchester.org/wp-content/uploads/sites/200/2022/03/Class-2-worksheets.pdf. Questions adapted from the Patient Health Questionnaire-9 (PHQ-9), developed by Spitzer, Williams, and Kroenke.

If the answer to several of these questions is yes (or even just one question marked with a * bullet point), recommend they see a mental health professional (psychiatrist, psychologist, therapist, or primary care provider) and offer to help them find resources or make appointments.

Grief and Depression

Grief and depression frequently coexist and it is not uncommon for grief to give way to depression, especially when the mourner feels isolated, unsupported, or overwhelmed. Some grieving individuals may develop clinical levels of depression—especially if they have a personal or family history of mood disorders,[47] or if the loss was traumatic or sudden. It is not uncommon to feel your faith has been shaken by the loss—if someone feels abandoned by God or life itself—the path of grief may become clouded by hopelessness and depression.

As a clinician, I've walked with many individuals facing both grief and/or depression—some grieving a tangible loss, others consumed by a sorrow that had no clear name. Both are forms of suffering, but they speak a different language to the soul and psyche. Therapeutically, grief is best met with presence and compassion, not with attempts to "fix" or erase pain. The goal is not to end grief but to accompany it, integrating the loss into a new narrative of life. Depression, while it needs the same presence and compassion, also needs a clear treatment plan and clinical intervention. In these clouded moments, it's essential for clinicians and loved ones to assess for signs of clinical depression: suicidal thoughts, feelings of worthlessness, persistent hopelessness,

[47] A family history of mood disorders, including major depressive disorder and bipolar disorder, is a well-established risk factor, suggesting a genetic and heritable component that may increase susceptibility to developing similar conditions.

and inability to function. It's also crucial to gently explore spiritual wounds that may be contributing to the depth of the suffering.

Closing Thoughts

Grief often keeps a healthy tether to our loss. Depression, on the other hand, can sever that connection — to others, to meaning, and sometimes to the sacred. As a therapist, our role is to discern the difference with care, so grief can be honored and depression can be treated — both with the dignity they deserve. Here are key takeaways:

- Grief is a normal, sacred response to loss. It is adaptive and changes over time.
- There is not a correct way to grieve. It looks different for everyone. Don't compare your grief experience.
- Simply stated, depression is experienced as feeling hollowed out, empty, or having a complete absence of feeling. This is different from grief, which involves having distinct feelings or reactions to a life experience and expressing them.
- Common with depression, suicidal ideation *always* needs to be taken seriously and attended to by a professional.
- Depression is very treatable. There are many resources that can be helpful to a person suffering depression. Psychologists, licensed clinical social workers, marriage and family therapists, psychiatrists, physicians, naturopaths, in-person or online support groups, and faith-based community groups are all valuable resources. Multiple professionals or support systems can collaborate for the care of a depressed individual.

Our Case Study: MARIA

To bring the concepts of grief and depression to life, the following case study illustrates how these experiences can manifest in a real person. The case example should highlight the nuances that distinguish adaptive grief, prolonged grief, and clinical depression. By exploring Maria's story, we can gain a deeper, more empathetic understanding of how loss and mood disorders affect daily life, relationships, and well-being, while also seeing the importance of appropriate assessment and intervention.

Case Summary 1

Maria, a 54-year-old woman, lost her husband of 30 years to a sudden heart attack. Eight months later, she continues to miss him deeply and experiences waves of sadness, especially during holidays and anniversaries. However, her grief has gradually changed over time. She is able to recall memories with both sorrow and warmth, and she finds comfort in reconnecting with her church group and gardening. While the loss remains painful, Maria expresses that she still has purpose in life and looks forward to spending time with her grandchildren.

Clinical impression: Maria's presentation reflects a process of normal, adaptive grief—painful but gradually integrating, without significant impairment in daily functioning.

Case Summary 2

Maria, a 54-year-old woman, lost her husband of 30 years to a sudden heart attack. Fourteen months later, her grief remains intense and overwhelming. She reports daily yearning for him, spends hours looking through his belongings, and avoids social gatherings because they feel "too empty" without him. She struggles to accept his death, stating, "Life has no meaning without him. I don't know who I am without my husband." Despite the passage of time, she remains preoccupied with the loss and unable to re-engage in life.

Clinical impression: Maria's symptoms meet criteria for Prolonged Grief Disorder (PGD), characterized by persistent, loss-focused distress and functional impairment well beyond the expected acute grieving period.

Case Summary 3

Maria, a 54-year-old woman, lost her husband of 30 years to a sudden heart attack. Eight months later, she reports feeling persistently sad and hopeless, not only when thinking about her husband but across all areas of her life. She has withdrawn from her church group and no longer finds pleasure in gardening. Her sleep is disturbed, appetite diminished, and concentration poor, affecting her ability to work. She expresses guilt for not recognizing her husband's symptoms sooner, describes herself as worthless, and admits to passive suicidal thoughts such as wishing she would not wake up.

Clinical impression: Maria's presentation is consistent with Major Depressive Disorder following bereavement, as her symptoms extend beyond grief into a pervasive depressive syndrome.

TABLE: MARIA SUMMARY COMPARISON			
TYPE	**Adaptive Grief**	**Prolonged Grief Disorder**	**Depression**
TIME SINCE LOSS	Eight months	Over 14 months	Eight months
EXPERIENCE OF LOSS	Still misses him, feels sad at times, but can recall happy memories	Intense daily yearning and preoccupation with husband, feels like has no meaning without him	Constant sadness and hopelessness, not limited to the loss of her husband
MOOD	Sadness comes in waves mixed with happy memories	Persistent loss-focused distress, no easing with time	Global low mood, loss of interest across all areas of life
DAILY FUNCTION	Rejoining gardening and church group, reconnects socially	Withdraws from friends and avoids reminders of husband	Struggles with work, can't enjoy gardening or social activities
SELF-PERCEPTION	"I'll always miss him but I can find joy in living"	"I don't know who I am without him"	"I'm worthless, life has no point"
TRAJECTORY	Gradual adaptation and integration of loss	Blocked adaptation; grief remains dominant and disabling	Ongoing pervasive depression requiring clinical intervention
CLINICAL TIMELINE	Grief is acute first few months with gradual change/lessen over time with some waves of intensity	PGD develops after at least 12 months (adults); six months (children and young adults)	MDD on set at any time; persistent symptoms every day for two weeks

CHAPTER 11
THIS CHANGES EVERYTHING

Your identity—how you view and value yourself—will change in grief. The person you were is different now. Your new identity includes the "old" identity, but you are no longer just that "old" identity. The challenge is to acknowledge this change. To realize this new identity is not a worse identity than you had before, but it has been altered. How will you allow this new identity to be expressed? For me, I wanted to honor Adam in a new and visible way, in a manner that was very different from the person I was before his passing. At age 54, I got my first tattoo.

Adam had many tattoos. I never understood his desire to put permanent ink on his body. I did not have tattoos primarily because I don't like pain. However, shortly after Adam's passing, I got my first tattoo, a "word cross" consisting of his initials at the top, in his handwriting, "Romans 5:8" as the cross beam and the verse Philippians 1:21 written out at the bottom. This was my way of honoring Adam's salvation and passion for ministry. I was mesmerized by this new ink on my left inner forearm. I would stare at it and remember my son. It would inspire me to live as Adam lived, full of passion for the gospel of Jesus.

After that first tattoo, I knew I wanted more. I started planning what the next tattoo would be. I chose "clouds with heaven's rays piercing through" as Adam too had this tattoo on his left arm. Wrapping around the "word cross," the rays of heaven with the clouds in the background became the canvas for a line from the song "Endless Praise" by Charity Gayle, "Standing with those who have heard well done!" This was my way of acknowledging what Adam already heard from Jesus in Heaven. I am standing with my son, who has finished his task on earth and has received his reward in eternal paradise as a faithful servant.

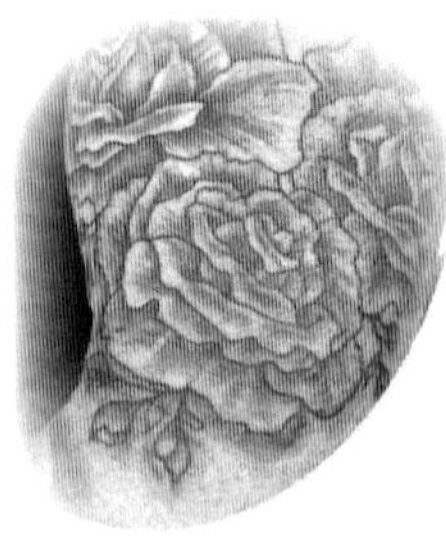

I had officially got the "tattoo bug." I began to consider what a full sleeve would look like. What tattoos did I want to add next? For my third tattoo, I also chose a tattoo that Adam had. I chose his first tattoo, "three roses." When Adam got this tattoo his senior year of high school, I asked him why he chose the "three roses" design; his spontaneously attributed it to his mom's birth flower, the rose, and the three children she had. Debbie and Aimee got this tattoo as well.

When I got the "three roses" done, I also added "Made in the Image of God" to my left exterior forearm. This design was a sticker we had made using Adam's handwriting, as we found this phrase in one of his journals. This was a powerful statement that I had focused on in dealing with my doubts in the goodness of God in Adam's passing. When I would look at that phrase, I had to confess that God made Adam in His image, which means God made Adam good but intentionally with a weak blood vessel in his brain. This tattoo became a statement of the faith I was seeking to grow in. Quickly my left arm was becoming the sleeve I envisioned it to be.

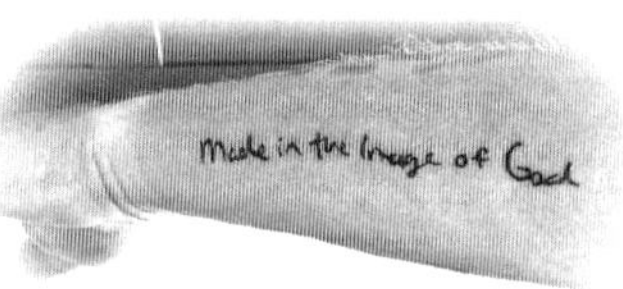

While on vacation with friends, I saw a waiter that had a tattoo on his elbow. It was not the design but the location that intrigued me. I began to draw a picture of Golgotha and the empty tomb combined as three crosses on a hill, with an empty tomb and the stone rolled away. The "open tomb" would be my elbow, with the hill, crosses and stone around it. I did not realize how painful getting a tattoo on my elbow would be; it felt like a blow torch fixated on my elbow for 2 hours. When finished, the "stone rolled" away looked like the moon, which confused people at first. So, I went back in to shop to have the stone darkened; more ink and more pain that resulted in the nerve in my forearm to go "dead" for a week. I thought I had nerve damage. The resulting picture is a testimony to the new life that Jesus gives as the resurrection is our hope for now and eternity. The resurrection has become the climax of the gospel story that I now tell. This is one of my favorite tattoos that I cannot see regularly but proclaims Christ was crucified and the tomb is empty to all who walk behind me.

As I contemplated how to finish my left-arm sleeve of tattoos, my daughter, Aimee, and I decided to get a butterfly tattoo, using Adam's thumb print as the left wing, and the Monarch Butterfly, common to our region of California, as the right wing. The butterfly was drawn casting a shadow, indicating the influence of Adam's legacy upon our lives. This tattoo has become my favorite as it represents Adam in the most unique way: his thumbprint is the picture of his life and what he continues to mean to me—his legacy for the gospel and its relevance in my world still today. This tattoo comes to life around me daily as the Monarch Butterfly makes its migration journey through my town in certain seasons of the year, and the butterfly is a tangible connection to Adam.

The last tattoo I placed on my left arm was again one that Adam had, a dove representing the Holy Spirit. In many ways, this tattoo is the capstone of the project. It is a constant reminder that it is only by God's power that I can live in the shadow of grief. It is by the Holy Spirit's guidance that I am able to navigate how to live rightly with my grief, expanding my capacity to grieve with hope. I was tempted to add the "clouds of heaven" around the dove and the "word cross" to produce a full sleeve of tattoos, but I decided against that idea (for now) to allow each tattoo to stand on its own, to be clearly seen. With the sleeve of tattoos now finished, I call this work "Adam's arm." Adam is identified with each of these tattoos in a very personal way. When I look at my left arm—I think of Adam and who I was as his father.

Debbie's Journey

Sharing my tattoos with people has become more of an experience than I anticipated. I originally decided to get them with the intention to honor the memory of Adam and the connection he and I shared. He called himself a mama's boy in a letter he once wrote to me, full of gratitude with sincerity of how he appreciated and needed me in his life. I wanted to show my gratitude and honor his life by getting tatted as he loved to do the same. I turned 52 the day after Adam passed, never did I expect to be drawn to get a tattoo so much. I had the desire to get one after he left this earth. I now see why, I needed a new connection to my son. This reminds me of the way God desires to connect with me every day! I have failed my Savior on this type of connection; I have confessed to my Lord that I will honor my son second and Him first! This is how I now show it, by my tattoo on my arm that has Adam's initials and Romans 5:8. I copied his roses tattoo onto my ankle that represents the three children I was gifted by God. I also tattooed an elephant on my left heel to represent the mourning I will always be in for my son. Elephants kick their left heels along the dirt while they mourn a loss of their own. I share this tattoo with my daughter Aimee along with the roses.

My counselor, remarking on my tattoos said, "If your left arm is about your identity with Adam… what is your right arm identifying?" I was not sure of what it should signify. The left right arm spoke volumes about an identity that was lost. My identity had been being a dad, Adam's dad. I invested significant hours, dollars, and energy into stewarding God's gift of Adam. I believe I did the job well. I took great fatherly pride in what God was doing through Adam. I did not take credit as I knew the path to righteousness that Adam took was perilous at times, and I give full glory and praise to God for what He alone could do and did. Yet, being Adam's father was a key part of my identity, and that identity took a painful hit when Adam suddenly died. The truth is I died that day too. That took a while for me to recognize as in my grief I kept trying to return to what was "normal," but now there was a new "normal." Who I am to be is no longer what I had been. I was lost in understanding clearly who I was now. My identity was adrift on an ocean of emotions and doubts.

That imagery of being adrift on the ocean, following the currents to an unknown destination became a vision of my new reality, my new identity. In faith, I was taking a new journey—one that I did not want to take but was on regardless. Therefore, my right arm has come to represent the "new journey" (the name I am giving this work in progress), with a series of tattoos in development to express the journey in a visual water scene. The primary tattoos are a series of Hawaiian design sea turtles, each representing a different member of my family. The sea turtle (*hono* in the Hawaiian language) has been my fascination when traveling around and snorkeling in Hawaii.

I remember being mesmerized in my first encounter swimming with a sea turtle. Watching the turtle glide effortlessly through the water. On one vacation we found a sea turtle resting place and Adam was able to quietly come alongside the turtles to take an amazing picture that has become one of my favorite memories of Hawaii. I have gone back to this beach since Adam's passing as a place of refuge and reflection, sitting alongside the turtles, praying as they slept. I have even been surprised by a sea turtle while snorkeling; he was so at ease around humans that he swam up behind me and I almost bumped into him unexpectedly. My love affair with the sea turtle continues to this day as I seek to make watching sea turtles in their natural habitat a priority for all vacation trips when possible. I have been captured by the beauty of their design. Turtle shells display a variety of patterns depending on the species and individual variation. While all turtles have a hard outer shell (carapace) and a bottom shell (plastron), the specific arrangement of scutes (the individual plates that make up the shell) can vary greatly. Some turtles have highly patterned shells with distinct shapes and colors, while others have more uniform or simple patterns.[48] It's the pattern on the shell that provides one of the quickest ways to identify the species of the turtle. I like to think the shell is the turtle's identity, which is why in my new tattoos each turtle's shell is unique to identify a specific family member. As I am currently working on this sleeve, the family shells are still being considered and refined. I started with my turtle, with a cross on its shell representing my faith in Jesus as the foundation for the "new journey." Debbie's turtle has a plumeria flower on its shell and will be the only tattoo I will get with color, to represent the beauty to be found in our new journey. Each family member (child, grandchild, son, and daughter in-law) will have a turtle swimming in the current of the

[48] Chen Nyok, "Shell Patterns and Identification," Turtle Conservation Society of Malaysia, (Oct. 26, 2009), https://www.turtleconservationsociety.org.my/shell-patterns-and-identification/.

new journey. To represent this current, a water scene will be shaded in with "He leads me" (from Psalm 23:2) written in Hebrew characters on my right wrist, all indicating the new journey we are on is our new identity.

Interestingly, sea turtles are by nature solitary animals, even anti-social. After birth, a young sea turtle does not usually gather with other turtles until it reaches mating age. I recently learned God created a sea turtle with the ability to live most of their lives under water. Sea turtles do not need to come to shore but will do so to rest in the warm sand to regulate their body temperature. It is at these moments you will see sea turtles clumped together for warmth and safety. What a beautiful picture of what we need: rest and safety. In this new journey of dealing with grief in expanding capacities, I have found the need to rest more and turn to trusted confidants for a safe haven to express my ideas, dreams, and ambitions for all God is doing in and through my life.

While sea turtles are not social with other sea turtles (except during mating season), sea turtles engage in various symbiotic relationships with other marine life, benefiting themselves and other species. These relationships range from mutualism, where both organisms benefit, to commensalism, where one benefits and the other is neither harmed nor helped. Examples include fish cleaning algae

off turtle shells, turtles eating sponges that inhibit coral growth and the "mowing" of the sea grass at the bottom of the ocean for the fish to feed. We see a strange relationship when turtles and monk seals share beaches for rest and warmth.[49] This is a beautiful picture of what the new journey will require, times of solitary movements but in corresponding harmony with other people around us who are on their journey also. While grieving has brought Debbie and I closer together, there are aspects each of us must do alone. We grieve differently so there is an acceptance to allow the other to "go off" and grieve alone as needed. Yet these relationships have a loving mutualism, doing life together. The new journey requires the symbiotic approach to life, realizing each person's experience in the "current" will be different. The key is not to allow the solitary life to lead to isolation. We must keep returning "home" to each other and to our foundation. Female sea turtles return to the same beach to lay their eggs as to where they were born. We too must return "home"; return to what is our core identity. The "new" identity of the new journey builds upon what is foundational to our old identity: the faith we had, the covenantal relationships we committed to. In this way, the old identity is not lost but honored as it creates the currents in which the new journey is taken.

Everything changes as some things are held onto. Ohana is another Hawaiian term meaning family, and family includes those not biologically connected but whom are brought into the circle of care. Family means you will not be forgotten. The Ohana of Hono (Family of Sea Turtles) is an oxymoron in nature but an intriguing picture to think about, as they would not all be sea turtles. The Ohana of Hono would include yellow tang fish who eat the algae and parasites

[49] Merge Gupta-Sunderji, "Seeking Out Symbiotic Relationships Can Make You a Better Leader," Merge's Blog, (Nov. 11, 2023), https://www.turningmanagersintoleaders.com/seeking-out-symbiotic-relationships-can-make-you-a-better-leader/.

on the turtle's shell. The Ohana would also be various fish and snails who hitch a ride on the back of a sea turtle. For our analogy's sake, the Ohana of Hono would be various individuals doing life in their own way but seeking to do it together as possible, benefitting from being with each other. This is the symbiotic nature of people grieving together. They will grieve differently but be able to sympathize with the basic needs of others grieving. For those who are grieving the loss of a loved one, it is important to remember that Ohana means "not forgotten." Please do not think that the reality of a new identity means those who are no longer physically present are forgotten. If anything, their loss is the greatest influence on the new identity. As we remember the important and best qualities of our loved one, these are included into the new identity formation. The love for the person who has passed will persist in the new journey, reflecting on behaviors and beliefs that sustain us. My new focus on the final resurrection that Jesus brings has shaped the hope my new identity is based upon. Before Adam's passing, my thoughts of Heaven were a simple cartoon in my mind, having no direct impact upon my previous identity. However, now my new identity is building upon my destiny in a resurrected body living eternal in Heaven alongside my loved ones. This is just one example of how the person we love but have lost a physical connection to is shaping our new identity.

FOR THOSE WHO HAVE BEEN CHANGED BY GRIEF

One of the most important "lessons" I have learned in my grief is that our identity is not simply the loss or the grief, but it is the resilient person God is working in us to be. Even though we continue to live in the shadow of grief and may always have this feeling about us, the shadow does not define us. The shadow is not our new identity.

So how do you respond when you feel as if the shadow of grief is not just the "new normal" but the new identity you are stuck with? First, you must consider if this is an identity issue or a depressive mental health state of mind. If you're feeling sad or down most of the day, for most days, over a long period of time, you may have persistent depressive disorder. It's important to talk to a healthcare provider if you have depressive symptoms. Medication, counseling, and healthy lifestyle choices can help make you feel better. Please see the previous chapter on how to properly address this chronic condition.

For those who are wrestling with the shadow of grief as an identity issue, remember you do not lack anything as you wait to be reunited with your loved one in Heaven! Your identity is still rooted in your identity as a child of God based on the forgiveness granted you by Jesus, sustained by His death and resurrection from the dead.

> *I always thank my God for you because of his grace given you in Christ Jesus. For in him you have been enriched in every way—with all kinds of speech and with all knowledge—God thus confirming our testimony about Christ among you. Therefore, you do not lack any spiritual gift as you eagerly wait for our Lord Jesus Christ to be revealed* (1 Corinthians 1:4–7, NIV).

God is enriching my new identity with new knowledge, enlarging my understanding of who Jesus is. I have been empowered by the Holy Spirit so I can endure until Jesus' return, and I am resurrected to be with Adam and all the saints. Building upon the work God is doing in your life, you must recognize the "Ohana" God has placed around you, the diversity of people who are grieving with and loving you. My new identity is my new journey that has me continuing Adam's legacy for the gospel by starting his foundation. The roles I play in the kingdom of God have been changed for the better for the work of God in and around due to my pain.

My new identity is one that has been created to comfort others. God never wastes my pain. In the sovereignty of God, I am His tool to bring compassion and comfort to others who are grieving.

"Praise be to the God and Father of our Lord Jesus Christ, the Father of compassion and the God of all comfort, who comforts us in all our troubles, so that we can comfort those in any trouble with the comfort we ourselves receive from God" (2 Corinthians 1:3–4, NIV). Notice how Paul described God, a God of compassion and comfort. The Greek word for *compassion* is literally translated "bowels," as it was thought this was where the heart of compassion resided.[50] It is a vivid picture of the intense feeling that it is often translated as "mercy," as this is what motivates someone to show mercy to another person. God is called the "Father of compassion" or "mercy" as He is the greatest example of love. The Greek word used in the New Testament for comfort always implies more than soothing sympathy. It has the idea of strengthening, of helping, of making strong.

God comforts us in all our troubles, in everything we experience—God comforts us as we truly want to be comforted when experiencing an awful, no-good, bad day. I have been a Fire Chaplain for over 30 years; starting the program for the Rancho Cucamonga Fire Protection District and later serving the Orange County Fire Authority as a battalion chaplain and eventually as the Senior Chaplain. In my service as a chaplain, I have been called to the homes of many people who lost loved ones to death, sitting with them in those first awful moments of grief. Never did I expect to be on the other end

[50] Strong's Lexicon, "G3628 – *oiktirmos*," https://www.blueletterbible.org/lexicon/g3628/kjv/tr/0-1/.

of this relationship. For the first time, when Adam died, I was the one needing comfort. I now know so much more clearly what others need in these crisis moments because of what I experienced, and I have been able to comfort others with greater empathy. The truth is—when we are grieving, we want someone who feels our pain with us, cries with us. We want someone who is present with us, even when it is uncomfortable. We want someone who is calm and peace-filled, to settle the chaos with our nature. We want someone who is able to lift us up and strengthen us to stand again.

God is the ultimate of all those qualities. I believe God grieves when bad things happen to us (Romans 12:19) as God is with us always, never leaves us or forsakes us (Hebrews 13:5); God gives us peace that transcends understanding (Philippians 4:7) and God empowers us to do more than we think we can (Ephesians 3:20). God walks with us in our grief so we can be comforted so we can comfort others. In my grief, I have come to the realization that Adam was given to Debbie and me as a gift to be stewarded, as most parents feel about their children. Just as Debbie and I stewarded Adam's life for the glory of God, Debbie and I are learning to steward Adam's death; that our grief has stretched us and taught us, and we must steward our grief for the benefit of others.

God can comfort us as He suffered in our place. "For just as we share abundantly in the sufferings of Christ, so also our comfort abounds through Christ" (2 Corinthians 1:5, NIV). This is the same idea Jesus expressed in John 16:33, "I have told you these things, so that in me you may have peace. In this world you will have trouble. But take heart! I have overcome the world" (NIV). David Guizk commented on this passage, "God may allow situations in our life where our only comfort is found through Christ. Sometimes we think the only comfort is found in a change of circumstances, but God wants to comfort us right in the midst of our difficult circumstances, and to do it through Christ."[51]

It is natural to wonder why God would allow the suffering in the first place. We would not need to be comforted if we did not experience suffering or grief. Like it or not, there are many New Testament passages that promise Jesus' followers will have suffering in their lives (John 16:33; 1 Peter 2:21; 4:12–13, 16; 2 Timothy 3:12). Jesus warned us not to worry about tomorrow, for each day will have enough trouble of its own (Matthew 6:34). God knows that because of the nature of life with free will, we will experience pain and hardships, but the great news is that pain is not wasted. You will suffer, but you will also be comforted so you can comfort others. This understanding allows our faith to enlarge so our new identity accepts (maybe not willingly) that our grieving will be part of our ongoing journey. Therefore, the key is to have the proper approach to suffering.

The ancient Greek word for *suffering* originally had the idea of actual physical pressure.[52] That is a great description of what extreme suffering and catastrophic loss is like; it's like a heavy weight on your chest and body that press you down until you feel like you can't go on. We must deal with this pressure, and God's desire is that we would be enduring through suffering. The ancient Greek word for *enduring* is not the idea of passive, bleak acceptance of a painful situation; such as being the victim in the dentist's chair,[53] we just sit there and take the pain of the drilling. This is not the endurance that the Bible is re-

---

[51] David Guzik, "Study Guide 2 Corinthians 1," (August 2022). https://www.blueletterbible.org/comm/guzik_david/study-guide/2-corinthians/2-corinthians-1.cfm?a=1079001.

[52] Strong's Lexicon, "G3804 – *pathēma,*" https://www.blueletterbible.org/lexicon/g3804/kjv/tr/0-1/.

[53] Guzik, "Study Guide 2 Corinthians 1."

ferring to, instead the Greek word for *enduring* better fits a marathon runner. This endurance is an attitude, the kind of spirit that can triumph over pain and suffering to achieve the goal. Enduring is active and focused on the outcome, winning the prize, which makes all the training and hardship worth the journey. While the prize for enduring grieving may be difficult to see on this side of Heaven, I can testify that I am a different person now and there are aspects of strength, character, and compassion in my life that are new. God is working in me to work through me. These are prizes that I am receiving that I did not even know I needed, but God did. God had a larger purpose in Paul's suffering than just working on Paul himself. "And our hope for you is firm, because we know that just as you share in our sufferings, so also you share in our comfort" (2 Corinthians 1:7, NIV). God brought comfort and salvation to others through Paul's sufferings. In the same way, when we endure hardships and share the comfort we received from God, it has a powerful effect on the lives of other people, producing a patient endurance when they go through hard times.

"But this happened that we might not rely on ourselves but on God, who raises the dead" (2 Corinthians 1:9b, NIV). As we endure the hardship and grow into our new identity, we are discovering that the true source of strength comes when we rely not on ourselves but on God, who raises the dead. Too often when life spins out of control, I try to stop the spinning with my power and strength. I do this when I ride the Teacups at Disneyland. I only ride this attraction because my family likes it, I don't like to spin, so I try with all my might to counter the spin. However, this usually ruins the fun for others and leaves me exhausted. These are the same results in my life as I rely on myself instead of God, fighting against what only God can accomplish. I strain unsuccessfully to steer my life back into what I deem is best, a return to what was. However, God is in the business of restoring things to life, it is what He is best at. Therefore, I need to stop trying to control the spin and allow God to do His work!

I returned to those dreaded Teacups at Disneyland a few days ago with my granddaughter, Adam's daughter. She loves the Teacups, so we rode them again. However, this time I did not become sick or dizzy on the ride because I was staring at my granddaughter the whole time; while watching the joy on her face I did not notice the world spinning around me. This was the secret—knowing where to look. In my spiritual journey, I have become fixated upon God's power for the resurrection of His people. This is our hope. Even though our resurrection is a future event, there is a sense in which the reality and power of the resurrection touches every day for the suffering Christian. As we know through the power of His resurrection we will also be blessed by the fellowship of His sufferings to endure our hardships. This promise is based on who God is. "He has delivered us from such a deadly peril, and he will deliver us again. On him we have set our hope that he will continue to deliver us" (2 Corinthians 1:10, NIV). Notice the pattern Paul gave us here, God "Who delivered us… delivers us… He will continue to deliver us." Paul knew that God's work in our lives happens in three different verb tenses: past, present, and future. Experiencing the power of the resurrection goes "hand in hand" with participating in suffering, as then our focus is on the hope of Heaven, this is the new identity that is truly worth living for.

TO THOSE WALKING ALONGSIDE SOMEONE WHO HAS BEEN CHANGED BY GRIEF

Those of you who are walking alongside someone who has been impacted by significant loss must accept the fact that all of this person's relationships have changed in some way: for better or worse.

Most likely the new nature of your relationship with this person will be more different from what you thought or were prepared for it to be. Instead of trying to force the previous relational dynamics to return, you must take what time or attention they can offer on their terms. This requires you to be patient and available. In my service as a fire chaplain, we have a phrase that defines and guides our actions: "be visible and available." This is the action of patiently waiting until the person is ready for you and desires what you have to offer.

"Be visible" does not always mean be physically present but rather finding subtle ways to let the person know you are thinking of them. One way Debbie and I let Adam's wife know we are present is we will reach out to her on an emotionally hard day with a simple text "love you." Often a day or two later, she will respond with a similar statement "love you." The key is that she knows we are present with her even if not physically in the room.

"Be available" means to let the person know, even nonverbally at times, that you are ready when they need you. After saying you are there for the person, make sure you are. When Adam's wife asks for anything from Debbie and I, we cancel what we have planned (if we are not out of town) and are present for her. We do reach out every few weeks or so to ask if there is anything she needs but then we wait for her response, which sometimes never comes. And that's ok.

You may be frustrated by the waiting. Your heart will ache to do more. You too will grieve what you have lost, not just your relationship with the one who has passed, but the emotional connection you had with those who have been left behind and are grieving. You will feel justified to encourage the grieving person to move on, but don't! I have often written a text to Adam's wife only to express my feelings and then deleted it before sending. The practice was for me. That I could acknowledge my pain and desire without forcing it upon the person who is already suffering more than I am aware of.

If you can maintain this willingness to be present on the other person's terms, you will see reconnection eventually, but it will still be different from what you had before. In some ways, the relationship will be stronger because it is founded on true empathetic love and not your needs being met. This is the greatest demonstration of love, to lay down one's life (your desires, your needs, your expectations) for the benefit of another (John 15:13). May God's love and comfort for you allow you to love and comfort the grieving heart on their terms as you accept that death has changed everything.

SECTION 4
ENLARGING YOUR CAPACITY TO GRIEVE WITH HOPE

We have come to the last section of the book but one that may seem to be far off in the processing of your grief. It is the "grieving with hope" that will pull you forward in your grief. Returning to our original analogy of grief as a ball in a jar (discussed in the Introduction), if you have been truly processing your grief, reacting, responding, and living in the shadow of grief, then your life (the jar) has become larger! It may not seem so to you, but you have greater capacity now to handle the grief and other aspects of life. This capacity will be experienced by the little moments of joy you begin to have regularly.

Your capacity has enlarged to take on responsibility for other people or projects. In time you will feel this enlargement as you grieve with hope, but it may be seen in you by others first. Close friends and family members will observe your enlargement and may even make comments you are not ready to hear but are true. You are moving on in your grief. Your living with grief will now include more than you thought you would have again. This is the new capacity you have to grieve with hope; a capacity to look forward to all that our hope in Jesus has secured for us. In this last section, we will discuss in detail all you have to look forward to in this hope!

CHAPTER 12
WHERE IS THE JOY?

The apostle James calls us to "Consider it pure joy, my brothers and sisters, whenever you face trials of many kinds (James 1:2, NIV). Can you really look forward to joy when you still feel such loss of your loved one? Can joy and grief coexist? I have wrestled with the concept of "joy" since Adam's passing. I have wondered how to consider it pure joy when facing trials. This challenge is at the very beginning of the James' epistle; it's verse 2! I was curious as to why James would make that his first thought. Perhaps a brief look at the life and faith of its author would help us understand. James was the half-brother of Jesus, who could not have been an easy older brother to try living up to. Imagine having the Savior of the world as your older brother; everything He did was literally perfect. It appears that James did not immediately believe his brother was the Messiah as he was most likely part of the family that came to stop Jesus from embarrassing the family (Mark 3), thinking He was mentally unstable. However, sometime during Jesus' ministry James became a believer that Jesus is the Messiah; James even received a special resurrection appearance of Jesus (1 Corinthians 15:7). This encounter created such strong devotion in James that he became a powerful teacher of God's truth.

We are not made aware of specific trials James faced apart from the general persecution the early church faced from the Roman empire and Jewish leaders. These first Christians were persecuted on every side, refused protection by the Jewish community, and they were exploited and abused by the Gentiles.[54] Church tradition tells us that James was martyred in Jerusalem by being pushed off the Temple wall. However, the fall did not kill him, and so he was beaten to death, as he prayed for his attackers.[55] I believe it is a safe assumption to say James had a difficult life, as James never claimed his birth family status, simply introducing himself as a "servant to God and of the Lord Jesus" (James 1:1). James did not use his family connection to benefit his life as he took on a role of a servant to his brother, calling him Lord. James was writing as a man who knew hardships to a people scattered around the world due to hardships. These people were acquainted with grief as they lost their jobs, their homes, and their loved ones because of their faith in Jesus. It is to these people that James said, "Consider it pure joy, my brothers and sisters, whenever you face trials of many kinds, because you know that the testing of your faith produces perseverance" (James 1:2–3, NIV). Notice James

[54] R. Kent Hughes, James: *Faith That Works, Preaching the Word* (Crossway, 2015), 17.

[55] David Guzik, "Study Guide James 1," (2022). https://www.blueletterbible.org/comm/guzik_david/study-guide/james/james-1.cfm?a=1147001.

highlighted the enlarging capacity to grieve with hope that these people have, "your faith produces perseverance."

Debbie's Journey

I never realized I was lacking in my love for God until my grief hit a huge low, when I wanted to give up. Let me be clear, not ever wanting to end my life, but I did in fact ask God to trade my life for Adam's. This was almost a daily conversation I had with God for the first two weeks my son was gone. He reminds me in Scripture that I need to persevere through this (James 1:12). My strength is His. My hope is in Him, as my comfort and peace come from Him. My faith in my Savior has grown through my grief and trials; this simultaneously increases the love I have for Him.

THE CONNECTION BETWEEN JOY AND PERSEVERANCE, AND FAITH AND HOPE

There is a direct connection to joy you will experience and the faith-produced-perseverance that becomes part of your journey. The joy is not in the trial itself. The joy is in the result of persevering through the trial. The person we are enlarged to be is worth the journey, no matter how difficult it is. That is the great news (I've said it before and I'll say it again)—God never wastes your pain! God ordained the number of days of Adam's life on earth. That means God knew exactly when my heart would break and my life would turn upside down. In God's sovereign power, God had a plan to use this pain for His good. Good for others and for myself. Remember God used Joseph's betrayal by his brothers to provide deliverance for God's people (Genesis 50:20) and God is using my pain to shape me to become more like Jesus (Romans 8:28–29). I am not a victim. I am a work in progress. Grief is the tool that God has chosen to use in my life for this moment. He is using other tools to chisel the hardness of your life away. This is why James said we can consider it "pure joy" when we face trials, because we can be confident that God is at work. This is where our faith rests.

Faith is shown in our deliberate and careful decisions to experience joy in times of trouble, focusing on what faith-produced-perseverance will lead to. When I was growing up, I was good at math but did not like doing math. My math scores earned me a seat in the highest math class my high school offered, "Advanced Topics." It was so advanced they did not know how to define it better. However, it was more than I could understand. Lucky for me, my dad was a card-carrying NASA rocket scientist. I would go to my dad for help on my math homework, just wanting the answer. Instead, my dad would give me a lecture on the math theory needed to understand the problem. All I wanted was an easier way out; my dad was determined to show me the process required. It was frustrating to endure, even painful at times, but the result was I was able to comprehend future problems. My "faith" in who my dad was and the belief he cared for me gave me the strength to endure those lectures. This is a picture of what God is doing in our grief. As we are processing our grief, we are just wanting the pain to go away. Yet God is wanting to use this moment for His purposes for us. For God knows the more tests we pass, the stronger we become, and the easier future hardships are. God used a lion and bear in the younger days of David's life as a shepherd to prepare him for the greatest threat he or Israel had ever faced. David confessed, "The Lord who rescued me from the paw of the lion and the paw of the bear will rescue me from the hand of this Philistine" (1 Samuel 17: 37, NIV). David was able to face the giant Goliath because he had faith-based optimism that was forged in the fire. Faith-based optimism can also be labeled "hope." To summarize, we can read James 1:2–3 as a call to endure hardships and grief because we can take joy in the hope that our faith-produced perseverance will lead to. This is the journey to enlarging your capacity to grieve with hope.

Most of us want to know where the journey will lead to before we start traveling. We care about the destination. If the destination is considered unworthy the effort, we will not embark on the journey. James tells us to preserve in the journey with grief because the destination is so worthy of the effort. "Let perseverance finish its work so that you may be mature and complete, not lacking anything" (James 1:4, NIV). The Greek word translated "mature" can also be translated "perfect." This is an important theme for James as he used this word seven times in this short letter; it means "wholeness."[56] In this context, it means living a completely integrated life, your actions are always consistent with the values and beliefs you have learned from Jesus. The enlargement of your capacity to do life despite grief is a completeness that does not come simply by the trials themselves, but rather by the perseverance in trials that produces maturity. In other words—it's all about how you respond to the hardship.

To endure the trial and grief requires more than simple willpower, it requires a new perspective—a wisdom of God. James is quick to point out that if you lack this wisdom, all you need to do is ask (verse 5). Now wisdom is different from knowledge. Knowledge is informational; it can be useful, but it can also be trivial. I have watched the television hit show "Jeopardy," marveling at the random knowledge required. I know people who love playing along with "Jeopardy," testing their knowledge, which is not bad, but it also does not seem very

[56] Strong's Lexicon, "G5046 – *teleios*," https://www.blueletterbible.org/lexicon/g5046/kjv/tr/0-1/.

helpful. God's wisdom is an understanding for living that surpasses earthly wisdom for it is meaningful and practical for both "here and now," and for eternity. God gives us wisdom—generously, without finding fault. These are two amazing qualities of God that are so unlike me. First, God gives us more than we need, He gives an abundance. Secondly, God does not judge the reason we need wisdom. He does not mock us for our lack of understanding. He does not give us a lecture that He's already told us once. The language James used in verse 5 tells us God is just waiting for us to ask, it literally reads "let him ask the constantly giving God."

James said to ask God for wisdom and then doubt what God has revealed is like being seasick (verses 6–8). I believe there is no worse feeling than being seasick, as when the best thing that can happen is to vomit, you know it's a terrible situation. I want to point out there is a difference between having doubts and questions about God, and the "double-minded man" James is referring to. If you have occasional doubts, God says ask for insight. In the past few years, I have wrestled with questions about God that I never considered before. In my anger at God, I asked questions that doubted His faithfulness. I wrestled with the good work that God was trying to do in my life. I felt like the father whose son was possessed by a demon and did not fully know what Jesus could do. Jesus challenged his faith and the father immediately declared, "I believe; help my unbelief!" (Mark 9:24, ESV). That man was not double-minded. He wanted to believe and declared his belief. His faith was weak, but it wasn't plagued with a double-minded doubt. The double-minded person James is referring to is the person who looks to God and then says I have no need of this. That believer is unstable in all they do, for God's wisdom is calling us to choose to trust God—that God is good despite my circumstance. God's wisdom allows me to see my hardships through a new perspective that helps me to persevere and produces spiritual maturity in me. I am a different, paradoxically more complete man now for having experienced such a deep loss in my life. This is the enlarging of my capacity to grieve with hope.

James concluded this introductory challenge with a promise. "Blessed is the one who perseveres under trial because, having stood the test, that person will receive the crown of life that the Lord has promised to those who love him" (James 1:12, NIV). Notice the motivation to persevere; it is love for God. When going through the trial, the feelings to "give up" can only be overcome by greater passion for something else, and that is a passion for an intimate relationship with God. Love is the greatest motivation to overcoming any challenge. When my daughter, Aimee, was ten she accompanied me on a mission trip to Costa Rica. It was the first time I was solely responsible for my daughter as my wife stayed home with Adam. One free day we all went hiking in the rain forest and my daughter badly twisted her ankle and she could not walk the remaining few miles back to the base camp. So, I put her on my back and began the grueling uphill journey home. My heart was pounding out of my chest. My breathing was labored. I was drenched with sweat. The younger high school boys all offered to carry Aimee, but I refused their help. I wanted to carry her regardless of the difficulty because I loved her more than anyone else around me. My love for her was my motivation to persevere in the difficulty. My love for my daughter was revealed in that effort.

Grief does that same work; it reveals what is real and already present. When going through a trail, my faith will be revealed, a faith that is already present in my life, and that faith is fueled by my love for God. My love for my son Adam is weighed and measured against my love for Jesus. If my love for my son is greater than my devotion to God, then I will struggle in the grief. If my love for God was less than anything this world offered, then I would always choose this world over God. However, that is a hopeless foundation for life as this world is for the short-term and God offers eternal life with Him and my loved ones. When I love God over all other things, I also receive back all that I also love, just not on the terms I may want (Matthew 6:19–20, 33). However, that is where a hope produced by faith leads me: to choose to live for a greater love for God. Undergirding this faith is an attitude of gratitude that empowers me to choose God during the trial.

FOR THOSE LACKING JOY

DEVELOP GRATITUDE: THE ATTITUDES THAT PRODUCE JOY

The apostle Paul gave us two challenges to embrace when going through trials. In the context of prayer, which is one of the first things any of us do when going through a hardship, Paul told us to be watchful and thankful. "Devote yourselves to prayer, being watchful and thankful" (Colossians 4:2, NIV). While we may not be able to change much about our difficult circumstances, Paul desired for us to change our perspective on our circumstances. When life beats us down, it is easy to take a discouraged posture, with our heads down, looking at life through smudged and dirty lenses, like my glasses as I try to type these words. Paul knew if we are going to overcome the hardships of life, then we need to change our perspective and that begins with how we pray. We are to pray with a watchful and thankful heart.

First, we are to be watchful, which means to pray with expectation of what God can do in the future. The famous missionary to India, William Carey, said "Expect great things from God—Attempt great things for God."[57] What would our prayers be if we prayed with great expectations of God and what God can do! Would our prayers be focused merely on our survival or would we pray for God's strength to thrive, to overcome our circumstances, and to do more than we ask for or imagine. This type of prayer is rooted in the reality that God's Spirit indwells now, and His power is at work within us (Ephesians 3:20). When I expect God to work, I am watchful for His activity, and that is when I see more of God's work in and around me. This new perspective of God's activity causes me to be thankful, which is the second aspect to my prayers I am to embrace.

The Scriptures are full of psalms, prayers, and stories of people giving thanks to God. However, one story reveals it is not easy to give thanks amid difficulty. I am thinking of 10 men who had been healed of leprosy by Jesus. Luke's gospel tells us of an incident Jesus encountered on his way to Jerusalem (Luke 17:12–19). On the outskirts of town, on the border between Samaria and Galilee, Jesus met ten men who were lepers. It was not unusual for these lepers to congregate with one another. They were outcasts from society and had no company other than other lepers. Lepers were required to shout out "unclean" so others could avoid contact and not contract the disease. These men could not worship in the Temple, live with their families, nor work a meaningful job. Their lives were being robbed of them, one day and one diseased body limb at a time. When Jesus appeared, they cried out for mercy. This word can also be translated "pity." These men are desperate for any help that would restore their lives to wholeness and return them to their families. Jesus responded with compassion and told them to go show themselves to the priest

---

[57] William Carey is widely quoted as saying, "Expect great things from God; attempt great things for God" in a sermon preached on May 31, 1792, from Isaiah 54:2–3.

(Luke 17:14). Notice He did not say, "I heal you" or make some grand divine motion. He gave them a choice to make. To leave and fulfill the Old Testament law to be reinstated to Temple worship. Luke recorded "as they went, they were cleansed." It was a choice of faith. These men would be cleansed and restored if they had the faith to obey Jesus. This is what is required in every difficult circumstance we find ourselves in, faith to obey. This is a visual picture of the exhortation of James 1:3–4; our faith brings us through the journey to wholeness.

The realization they were healed came on the journey to the Temple; but while all ten men were healed, only one returned to give thanks to Jesus. It does cause us to wonder why only one returned and not all ten. I think some of them did not recognize they had been healed already; they have lived for so long in the difficult circumstances they may not have known what the healing would bring. I think others had endured the suffering of the disease so long they just wanted to get back to what they had lost, so the quicker they got to the Temple, the quicker they could return to their families. Could you blame them for wanting to go straight to the Temple? Or maybe, because Jesus did not do the healing the way they expected, they did not realize what Jesus had done for them. But "one of them, when he saw that he was healed, returned, and with a loud voice glorified God" (Luke 17:15, NKJV). This man praised God with "a loud voice." Think about it, what better expression should there be than loud shouting of praise when you realize you have been given your life back. I naturally have a loud voice; my wife often tells me to be quieter. In this situation, the healed leper has every right to be as loud as he possibly could be. Jesus commends this Samaritan, highlighting God's grace and mercy are given to all people, saying his faith has healed him. This is in addition to being physically cleansed, he has been fully healed of all emotional and spiritual brokenness as well. The healed leper's faith was demonstrated in both his demonstrative praise and in his choosing to show gratitude for what Jesus had done for him, and it restored him to wholeness.

The point of Jesus' story is for us to be like the one healed leper who made the choice to return to Jesus in thankfulness. This reveals that gratitude is a choice we make in our daily lives, regardless of the circumstances. I don't know about you, but when I've read this story of Jesus' healing, I have always thought what jerks those other nine healed lepers were, but then I realize how often I am just like them: forgetting to thank God. I think it's because I am so consumed with my problems, that when God's goodness comes in other forms than what I was hoping for—I miss it, and therefore I am not thankful as I should be. When God does heal me as I need, I too often rush onto the next moment of life. Gratitude requires us to pause, to remember where we were in our previous difficult situation, and to recognize the growth, the healing, and the changes God has brought into our lives. This produces a wellspring of thankfulness, even joy, within us. Thankfulness that we share in prayers, as Paul commanded, with the God who is enlarging our capacity to grieve with hope.

In this way, we counter the pain of our loss with gratitude. Gratitude reminds of what God has done so we live in expectancy of what God can continue to do. This produces a faith-based optimism, that we have already discussed, which creates our strong foundation of hope. To help me be grateful, even when I do not feel like it, especially in times of pain, I use a prompt as a spiritual discipline to pray prayers of gratitude. As I mentioned briefly before, whenever I see a butterfly I stop, pause, and reflect on what God has done recently in my life. I begin the prayer by thanking God for Adam, naming something I remember about him, and then I name one other thing I can be thankful for. This practice has been powerful in my life to turn my perspective in hardships to hope-filled faith steps. The prayers of gratitude have produced a thankfulness that has helped me rise out of depressive modes and stave off the questions of doubt with new evidence of God's work. The butterfly prompt to pray prayers of gratitude may be the single most effective response to grief that I have practiced helping me process my deep grief in losing Adam.

Debbie's Journey

I mentioned a letter Adam wrote to me in the last chapter, this letter was full of his gratitude toward me as his Mom. This kid of ours knew what it meant to be grateful! He showed his gratefulness to God in ways I knew didn't come from our parenting but only from God. I imagine Adam showing his gratefulness to God in this letter to me. This is an example to me to be grateful in all circumstances of my life.

Remember, gratitude is a choice. No matter how hard the journey is, I am learning I can choose to be grateful. Using my prompts, I choose to pray prayers of gratitude, forcing my perspective to change to the good that God is doing around me. "Rejoice always, pray without ceasing, give thanks in all circumstances; for this is the will of God in Christ Jesus for you" (1 Thessalonians 5:16–18, ESV). Notice, we don't give thanks for everything, but rather in everything. I am learning I can give thanks in all circumstances because as a Christ-follower, my joy isn't based in circumstances, but in God. Circumstances change, but God doesn't. Through this spiritual exercise I can enlarge my capacity to grieve with hope as I know God is still good and working His grace in me. This is the wisdom of James 1, that like the Pilgrims, when the journey is not what we want it to be, we stay focused on the promised result. Gratitude is the attitude that empowers us to endure every circumstance.

HOW CAN I GIVE THANKS IN EVERY CIRCUMSTANCE?

I can give thanks in every circumstance because of what I know. I know God sees it all (Psalm 139:7–12; Hebrews 4:13). I know He cares (Matthew 6:30–34, 10:29–31; 1 Peter 5:7). God knows my name (Isaiah 43:1; Psalm 91:14; John 10:3). I know He can help (Isaiah 41:10, 13). He has the power to change the situation; He can turn it around (Proverbs 3:5–7; John 16:33; 2 Corinthians 12:9). I know God has a purpose behind every problem (Romans 8:28–29; Jeremiah 29:11–13). I know that I will be rewarded in Heaven if I respond correctly (Matthew 5:12; 6:4; Colossians 3:23–24). I know all these things so even in the dark days I can give thanks in every circumstance. Paul knew what it was like to go through hardship.

> *Five times I received at the hands of the Jews the forty lashes less one. Three times I was beaten with rods. Once I was stoned. Three times I was shipwrecked; a night and a day I was adrift at sea; on frequent journeys, in danger from rivers, danger from robbers, danger from my own people, danger from Gentiles, danger in the city, danger in the wilderness, danger at sea, danger from false brothers* (2 Corinthians 11:24–26, ESV).

Therefore, Paul was teaching from experience when he instructed the young church in Thessalonica, that when we rejoice in all circumstances we are tapping into an incredible spiritual power. Here is a list of practices that Debbie and I did to increase our gratitude in difficult circumstances.

PRACTICES TO BE THANKFUL IN DIFFICULT CIRCUMSTANCES ...

1. Find a prompt to pray spontaneous prayers of gratitude (as detailed above).

2. Every day, say aloud three good things that happened. A study cited by Harvard Medical School showed that expressing thankfulness has an impact on our emotions. They found, "After 10 weeks, those who wrote about gratitude were more optimistic and felt better about their lives."[58] This is the impact of worshiping in community. I can declare my thanksgiving during the struggle through song and prayers, with the encouragement of my spiritual community.

3. Keep a gratitude journal. Make a list of how God and others have been of help to you. This practice allows you to look back weeks, months, and even years later to remember how God has been good to you. Matthew Henry, the famous Bible commentator, was robbed of his wallet once. He wrote in his diary that night all the things he was thankful about:[59]

   - First, that he had never been robbed before.
   - Second, that though they took his wallet, they did not take his life.

[58] Harvard Health Publishing, "Giving Thanks Can Make You Happier," August 14, 2021, https://www.health.harvard.edu/healthbeat/giving-thanks-can-make-you-happier.

[59] Billy Graham, "Answers," Billy Graham Evangelistic Association, https://billygraham.org/answers/how-can-i-be-thankful-even-when-life-is-hard.

- Third, because even though they took it all, it wasn't very much.
- Finally, because he was the one who was robbed and not the one who was robbing.

4. Savor the good moments. Debbie and I have found that lingering over a good meal or a beautiful sunset has a positive impact on our emotional wellbeing. I have sat in these wonderful moments and said, "Thank You God for _________." In times of grieving, too often life becomes a blur, and I have not wanted to remember the details. Gratitude is all about pausing to take in the good of any moment, regardless of how difficult the circumstance is. Savoring is intentionally allowing all your senses to be tantalized with new sensations of goodness.

5. Memorize God's Truth to verbalize in the hard times. I have continued my spiritual discipline to read and reflect on God's Word every morning. This allows me to hold onto His promises throughout the day, speaking truth when I need to hear it again. Remember even the Psalms of Lament end with a renewed vow of praise. Psalm 121:1–2 is a great promise; say it repeatedly: "My help comes from the Lord, who made heaven and earth" (verse 2, ESV). I have made promises like this a declaration to God before I even get out of bed in the morning. Remember, Jesus endured hardships for you, therefore turn to Him in truth. "For we do not have a high priest who is unable to sympathize with our weaknesses, but one who in every respect has been tempted as we are, yet without sin. Let us then with confidence draw near to the throne of grace, that we may receive mercy and find grace to help in time of need" (Hebrews 4:15–16, ESV).

FOR THOSE WHO ARE WALKING ALONGSIDE SOMEONE IN GRIEF

GENTLY REMIND THE PERSON OF THE GOOD IN LIFE

Depending on your level of connection to the person, share your perspective of the good you see in them, the growth of their character, the steadfastness of their faith. The affirmation I received from others was especially meaningful as they commented on the perseverance and authenticity I displayed. Others commented they could see the change in my preaching, adding a level of depth and relevancy to my explanation and application of God's Truth. It is important to be sensitive to share this perspective later in the person's journey with grief. I have intentionally placed this discussion in the last section of the book as this is something the person may not be ready to receive until after the first anniversary of their loved one's passing.

REMEMBER THE HOLIDAYS AND KEY DATES ARE ESPECIALLY HARD

Send gift cards for meals. Share prayers rooted in Scripture. Be sensitive in what is said, as the person does not need to be reminded this is a difficult season, they simply need to hear you love them and are thinking of them. Don't expect anything in return or even to have the gift acknowledged; remember it's not about you at this moment.

This step is especially hard for extended family members who have traditions that are no longer honored or participated in. Debbie and I always invite Adam's wife and his daughter to join us at the holidays, but we understand the times she is unable to accept. We don't press. We grieve their absence alongside Adam's, but this is the season we are living in. We believe in time, as our capacity to grieve with hope expands, we will find new ways to include them in our lives. We long for that day to come.

The good news for both the grieving heart and those walking alongside them, is eventually the sun does rise again. I finish this chapter, writing before the sun raises in Kauai, Hawaii. For those of you familiar with this island, you will know it is populated and has its time regulated by roosters crowing. Everywhere you go—there are roosters. Even now, I know the sun is about to rise because I hear the roosters crowing. It's a great sound. One that calls me to a new day of activity. This is the call of gratitude, beckoning you to joy through endurance of the trial at hand. May each of us look back with gratitude and acknowledge James was right to challenge us to "Consider it pure joy, my brothers and sisters, whenever you face trials of many kinds, because you know that the testing of your faith produces perseverance" (James 1:2–3, NIV).

CHAPTER 13
TURN TO GOOD

BEWARE OF DISCOURAGEMENT

In the relentless presence of grief, there will be a moment where discouragement will creep into your life. You have endured challenges. You have overcome depression. You have faithfully sought after God and surrendered to His purposes. You have sacrificed for your family and others who are grieving alongside you. Yet, it does not seem to be enough. Grieving with hope does not mean life becomes easier; in fact, the length of the journey still to come can be discouraging. There have been moments in my grieving my son that I felt as if God owed me something. As if I deserve recognition for how I have grieved well the loss of Adam. To be honest, I would rather have my son back and not have to enlarge my capacity to grieve with hope. In these moments I wonder if this journey will ever be worth the effort. That's discouragement. The questioning of the process that results in a disengagement with the journey. Discouragement is the downhearted mindset that cancels out the goodness I have experienced in the past couple of years since Adam's passing. Discouragement is disempowering the very work God is doing and seeking to expand in my life.

When we have these emotions and feelings, the question is, "Is there a way to experience these emotions and still reflect our faith in God?" In practical terms, how can we overcome the damaging effects of discouragement? I call this effort, "Turn to Good." It is not that my loss will become good, but I turn my thinking toward practices that develop good within my life again. This is not looking for the "silver lining" nor is it simply positive thinking. Turning to good is facing my heartache and discouragement head-on, seeking God in the moment, and working to create long-lasting goodness in the world.

Not all spiritual people overcome discouragement. The story of Elijah is an example of how not to handle discouragement. He went from the highest of highs and great spiritual victory to overnight feeling discouraged to the point of calling it quits, literally wanting to die. In 1 Kings 19, we are told about the attack against Elijah by Queen Jezebel. Queen Jezebel was such a wicked woman that she has become synonymous today with a woman that leads someone to ruin. Ironically her name means chaste or modest although the idolatry she led the country into rebellion with involved the most sensual of acts. She took the attack on the prophets of Baal, led by Elijah (1 Kings 18), very personal, as these prophets were supported by the royal treasury and ate at her royal table. Elijah had exposed the lie that Baal was no god, rather he was a powerless idol that gave the people permission to do whatever perversion they wanted. In response, Jezebel threatened to kill Elijah. What timing. Elijah had just seen a great victory of God and probably thought this would bring about the salvation of the whole nation, and yet he was immediately met with this threatening challenge. Instead of joy, he experienced discouragement.

Discouragement will come at us because we live in a broken world. Notice the effects of discouragement in Elijah's life. "Elijah was afraid and ran for his life. When he came to Beersheba in Judah, he left his servant there, while he himself went a day's journey into the wilderness. He came to a broom bush, sat down under it, and prayed that he might die" (1 Kings 19:3–4 NIV). In these verses we see discouragement's impact and the drastic steps it may lead us to take in response.

DISCOURAGEMENT'S FIRST NEGATIVE IMPACT: FEAR

Elijah took the threat seriously and reacted in fear (1 Kings 19:3). There is a time to be afraid. In true emergencies we must make quick, life or death decisions; the fear we sense is an important alarm to the real danger we are facing. Emergencies are rare, yet many of us live in a constant crisis mode, consumed by the fear of what could happen. After the loss of Adam, once the "emergency" passed and our family began the long road of living in the shadow of grief, I was paralyzed by all scenarios that were now possible—playing the horror movies of greater loss in my mind. By responding to each new experience in a fearful position we spend a lot of emotional energy and mental capacity focused on a reality that is not yet. Fear makes us overthink situations and react without good judgment to keep events at bay that are not yet part of our lives. This is the absolute worst time to make an important decision; whenever we act out of our fear, we usually end up making a bad decision.

DISCOURAGEMENT'S SECOND NEGATIVE IMPACT: ABANDONING OUR CALLING

Elijah ran away in fear (verse 3). Elijah ran far; Elijah went about 80 miles south to Beersheba. Elijah's fear had caused him to abandon the work God had for him, the discipling of the people of Israel after they repented and returned to worshiping God. However, Elijah was absent from this duty. He had given up the high calling God had presented him with. Elijah ran because he was solely focused on himself and his position. He could not see who else was standing beside him, faithful to God. Elijah did not take any time to receive counsel on what he should do next or prepare the people for his absence. He simply ran and left behind a work of God that needed his involvement.

DISCOURAGEMENT'S THIRD NEGATIVE IMPACT: EXTREME INAPPROPRIATE THOUGHTS (SUICIDE)

In 1 Kings 19:4, we are told that after running for 80 miles, Elijah ran some more. He ran to the point of physical exhaustion and emotional depletion. He ran until he was at the end of his resources, and he simply prayed to die. "I have had enough, Lord," he said. "Take my life; I am no better than my ancestors" (NIV). Elijah was a man of prayer; he prayed to make the rain and the dew stop for three and a half years, and then he prayed to make it start again. Now he prayed that he might die. Elijah's faith had crumbled to the point where he had had enough. He could not fathom how any good could come from this moment, so he entertained a fatalistic solution. Elijah's thoughts were on his own unworthiness, "I am no better than my fathers!" (verse 4, ESV). Instead of remembering God's faithfulness displayed just days prior on Mount Carmel, Elijah was consumed with his own shortcomings, no longer desiring to continue under the burden of this broken world.

Notice how God responded to Elijah's discouragement. God cared for Elijah. God gave Elijah the gift of sleep (1 King 19:5). Elijah was physically exhausted and overwhelmed; God knew Elijah needed to rest his body and mind. When we are anxious, we can't sleep. Psalm 23 states that God leads us beside quiet waters as that's when we are able to rest. Secondly, God cared for Elijah's other physical needs by giving him food and water, twice, to strengthen him for the journey ahead (1 King 19:6). God knows the journey is too much for you. The long road of living in the shadow of grief is something we cannot do on our own. We cannot do God work in man's strength. The path God has for us will discourage us if we try to do this on our own. The result of God's caring for Elijah in this moment of discouragement is that Elijah "went in the strength" (verse 8, ESV). God prepared Elijah for the journey ahead, as Elijah traveled 200 miles in 40 days, from the wilderness outside Beersheba to Mt. Horeb, also known as Mt. Sinai, to be with God. The message to Elijah is clear, God will meet us in our discouragement and empower us for the journey ahead. We are not destined to stay discouraged. The events of life may be disheartening, and we may be discouraged by the loss and challenging situation we find ourselves in, but it does not have to remain that way.

When Elijah meets with God on God's mountain, God has a simple question for Elijah, "What are you doing here?" (1 Kings 19:9, NIV). This was NOT where God wanted Elijah; he ran in fear from his calling to confront the wickedness of a nation. Now Elijah was 280+ miles away from where God had put him. The queen's threat did not come as a surprise to God, just as my grief did not shock God either. I believe even Elijah's discouragement was understandable to God, as God knows the tragic events of life take a toll upon our wellbeing. That is why God ministered to the physical needs of Elijah. What is most important for us to consider is the response we give in the discouragement. Elijah's response to God's inquiry was to have a pity party. To Elijah—and many servants of God since—it seemed unfair that a faithful servant of God should be made to suffer. Discouraging times make God's servants feel more isolated and alone than they truly are. What may seem out of place in the story is that God allows Elijah to vent his frustrations. God knew what the discouraged Elijah needed; he needed to be with the Almighty. In Elijah's discouragement, God invited Elijah into His presence (1 Kings 19:11–13). Elijah accepted God's offer to experience His presence. As Elijah stood outside on that mountainside, God was not in the dramatic forces of nature, but rather God was in the gentle whisper of His voice. This is how He deals with us in our brokenness—with a gentle revelation of Himself, for that is enough.

Afterwards, God asked Elijah the same question, "What are you doing here?" But Elijah gave God the same response, another pity party (1 Kings 19:14). Being in God's presence did not change Elijah's mindset nor emotional state. I know my discouragement has become dangerous to my wellbeing, and that I am in trouble spiritually and emotionally, when I am in God's presence, whether it be in worship at church or an amazing ministry activity, and I am numb to it. The presence of God does nothing to change my perspectives. The discouragement at this point has taken root and blinded me to what God is doing around me. Elijah was blind to the 7,000 other followers of God who had remained faithful despite the threats of the prophets of Baal (1 Kings 19:18). David Guzik noted in his Bible study guide, "Strangely, the reasons Elijah provided were actually important reasons for him to remain alive. If he really was the last prophet or believer alive, should not he seek to live as long as possible? If the enemies of God, like Jezebel, wanted him dead, should he not seek to defeat her wicked will? Elijah here powerfully showed the unreasonable nature of unbelief and fear."[60] Discouragement tempts us to give into the fear and irrational thoughts and run from the work God desires to do through us.

In these desperate moments of discouragement we must look for God in the pain, chaos, and confusion. This is what Elijah did not do. He did not take a moment and look through the lenses of faith for divine activity. Paul challenged us to remember that "we live by faith, not by sight" (2 Corinthians 5:7, NIV). The context of this exhortation is when circumstances are unclear or challenging, followers of Jesus ground their decisions, hopes, and daily lives in their faith in God's character and unseen plan. We can live this way because God is active around us as His Spirit within us guarantees what is to come, our eternal destination of Heaven (2 Corinthians 5:5). If we live by faith, not in response to the circumstances of our present lives, then we act as God is still powerful, active, loving, and wise. Therefore, as we turn to the good, we look for God in the moment. This allows us to see how God is responding in our discouraging situation.

Debbie's Journey

Turning to good for me required that I would depend on my foundational relationship with the Lord. He is who has been sustaining me through my grief and showing me His goodness in our family. I remember the day our granddaughter was born. We had just received a call and went to visit her and her mom in the hospital. Praying the whole way there, I heard God tell me that this gift is from Him. She is His just as her dad was. Immediately, I be-

[60] David Guzik, "Study Guide 1 Kings 19," (2002), https://www.blueletterbible.org/comm/guzik_david/study-guide/1-kings/1-kings-19.cfm?a=310001.

came emotional knowing that every child is ultimately HIS! This is good news! Our granddaughter is who I think of when I need to see the good in this world.God reminds me daily of how good He is in so many practical ways. I just must be aware because they are all around me.

When God heard of Elijah's persistent discouragement God responded two ways. First, God gave Elijah a job to complete. God was not finished with Elijah, and He gave Elijah a special task to complete. However, sadly this task was the beginning of the end of Elijah's calling as a prophet of the Lord. When we are going through severe discouragement, change is required. Either I need to change my mindset through rest, renewal, and refocusing on God or God will change my calling for me. This was the second response from God; God released Elijah from his calling and had Elijah anoint his successor (1 Kings 19:15–16). God had a plan for a new king who would bring justice and a new prophet that would proclaim His presence to the people of Israel.

In God's anointing of Elisha as the next prophet of God, Elijah was given two very important tools to overcome his stagnant discouragement: a friend and a purpose. First, Elisha would become Elijah's companion over the next few years. Remember, Elijah's greatest complaint was that he was alone in his faithfulness to God; but Elijah would be alone no more. 1 Kings 19:21 tells us that Elisha responded wholeheartedly to his commissioning by Elijah, and "he set out to follow Elijah and became his servant" (NIV). Elijah and Elisha worked together for approximately six years, providing Elijah the fellowship he needed to regain his faithful footing before God. Elijah continued to serve as a prophet of God after this mountain top experience with God. However, his purpose changed to mentoring Elisha and preparing him for succession as the prophet in Israel. Elisha's role involved serving Elijah and learning from him before Elijah's miraculous departure from Earth. The key takeaway to learn from Elijah's discouragement is that God meets us amid discouragement; God is working around us, therefore, when we can't sense Him, we must look for His activity.

HOW DO WE OVERCOME DISCOURAGEMENT WHEN CHALLENGED?

SEEK REST

We must respond as God directed Elijah to do. First, seek rest. While this is not necessarily the highest priority when dealing with discouragement, it may be the single best step you can take. Too often in our journey with grief, our sense of duty keeps us engaged longer than we should be in activities and we are living on adrenalin. When a moment of pause comes, the realization of our discouragement in our circumstances becomes a tidal wave that sweeps over us. Regular rest renews our body and mind for the difficult journey of dealing with grief that still lays ahead of us. Sleep research shows in the Dream cycles we process the events of our lives and categorize the memories.[61] This nightly work is often referred to as memory consolidation, and it involves transforming unstable, newly encoded

[61] S. Scarpelli, C. Bartolacci, A. D'Atri, M. Gorgoni, and L. De Gennaro, "The Functional Role of Dreaming in Emotional Processes," *Frontiers in Psychology,* 2019 Mar 15;10:459.

information into stable, long-term memories.[62] We must admit the "journey ahead of us is too much for us" and heed the angelic calling to rest. Ask yourself, "what can I stop doing for a short time to gain time back to rest?" I keep a glass ball on my desk as a reminder there are some things I cannot drop, but some I can. In seasons of discouragement, many things can be dropped to create space in your life for the journey ahead; these include appointments that scream "urgent" but are not important. You will be most tempted to drop the practices that are important but not urgent as these seem to be negotiable but resist the urge. The following practices are essential in dealing with discouragement.

DEVELOP NEW PERSPECTIVES

Elijah lost sight of all God had just done on Mount Carmel as well as the 7,000 others who were following God. Discouragement had blinded Elijah to the work of God. When we are grieving and facing even small challenges daily, we experience a "death by a thousand papercuts." The result is a lack of joy in our lives and a failure to thrive in our daily wellbeing. The constant struggle to find joy in our moment is the path discouragement takes us down. A spiritual practice we have discussed in this book previously that is worth emphasizing again is the practice of prayers of gratitude. Use spontaneous triggers, such a seeing a butterfly, to cause you to mentally pause and name the good that God is doing around you. We have already discussed this in detail, so that is all I will say on this practice, except to remind you of its power to help you overcome discouragement and restore the joy of God within you.

---

[62] M. Ahsan, "Role of Sleep in Memory Consolidation," *News Medical Net*, Oct 12, 2022.

Debbie's Journey

Taking the needed time to reflect helps me to also see goodness in my life and have clarity as to how God may be working. Since our loss of Adam, we have had many more trials in our lives. I could not survive these without the Word of God! His Word leads me, disciplines me, and brings me joy and peace. God's promises and character throughout His Word is what gives me hope.

DEVELOP HEALTHY RHYTHMS

There are great benefits to nutritional eating patterns with appropriate proportions and exercise in small 30-minute increments. Taking a short walk, both clears the head and gets the heart pumping; walk until you start to sweat as this is a good sign your body is working. The last rhythm is to stay in God's presence through spiritual practices such as Scripture meditation and prayerful responses. God's presence and "still small voice" is like the radio waves that are all around us and passing through us with music, sport scores, and news; we just need to tune our radio to the right frequency to experience them. We need to regularly participate in worship with God's people, read the Bible daily, and play worship music at home to focus on the truth of God's activity in and around us.

DEVELOP A SPIRITUALLY HEALTHY COMMUNITY

Another practice to overcome discouragement is to develop a spiritually healthy community to be with. This will be a much smaller group of people than your participation in a worship service, perhaps even smaller than your Bible study group that you meet with. While both gatherings are good, as mentioned in other chapters of this book, you will need a few individuals who are committed to you and your wellbeing. Elijah needed Elisha to continue moving forward. With Elisha, Elijah was able to serve God another six years, when just before, on his own, he was not desiring to live another day. Do not overlook the power of the empathy of others to help you overcome the waves of discouragement.

HAVE A NEW TASK TO FOCUS UPON

This could be a hobby that you enjoy or a new responsibility that gives you a sense of renewed purpose. God responded to Elijah's pity party by giving him specific tasks to do; these gave him hope that the future would be different. My friend Albi wrote me recently,

> *In my opinion, I think we forget that we are all created for a purpose. This purpose goes beyond just what we can see, touch, or feel, but that there are spiritual things that are happening as well. God wanting to transform us, but we need to see this transformation through spiritual eyes, so we can actually change our thinking, change our feeling, change our actions and how we respond.*

There is a connection between living purposefully and the ability to change how we feel. In the loss of a loved one, we may have also lost our purpose. The value we see in ourselves may have been directly connected to our loved one. Who we are and what we are meant to be and do has been changed. One way to restore this value is to discover a new task that gives purpose to our days.

In addition to new fun hobbies that restore your joy, I would suggest you also try these two new tasks, rich in purpose, that are worthy of your focus and time as you to turn to Good.

1) Developing the legacy of our loved one. The memories of your loved one will continue to live as long as you give them space to be honored. Think about the good qualities and impact your loved one had and consider how you could develop these to be the legacy of your loved one. Some grieving parents use their energy to raise awareness and funds to defeat the disease that took their child's life to spare the pain of loss for other families. Other people seek justice for the wrongful death of their loved one. I would encourage you to take a different approach. What is something your loved one did that was good and made a difference? How can you continue that quality or effort in activities or communities in honor of your loved one?

Adam is remembered as someone who made others feel seen, loved, and cared for—reflecting the heart of Jesus. I often share Adam's journey from a struggling teenager to a devoted youth pastor, remarking at the passion he showed in sharing the gospel with students. Adam's wife, key mentors, and his family came together to discuss how we could help the "next Adam" to continue Adam's legacy. I have already shared that we began the Adam Keehn Foundation[63] as a faith-based nonprofit organization dedicated to supporting and empowering young youth pastors as they lead students to the gospel of Jesus. This was established in memory of Adam, to carry forward his legacy by equipping new leaders with the tools and encouragement they need to thrive. As I participate in the coaching of young youth pastors, I can see the trajectory of what Adam would have done, and I beam with pride knowing Adam's story is not finished. You can get involved by requesting ministry coaching or resources and financially supporting this work by going to our website: adamkeehnfoundation.com.

2) Helping others in their grief. I share this last task with a word of caution as you may not be ready to listen to other people's story of

---

[63] Adamkeehnfoundation.com.

loss for some time. However, you now have a unique perspective into grieving. Your experience has given you knowledge of what another person may experience and, potentially, expect in the journey ahead. I was contacted by a grieving dad who tragically lost his daughter less than a year after Adam died. I listened to him. I cried with him. I was reliving those terrible first feelings all over again. While I was able to empathize with him at a deep level, I was too new in the journey myself to offer anything but tears. Since that first meeting, I have met with this dad a few times and have been able to share more helpful thoughts as I am further along the road of grief. It is important to remember that although our experiences may be like another person who has lost a loved one, there are enough differences in our journeys that we cannot make judgements about what this person needs. The newly grieving person will come to you with questions, looking for hope and guidance; you should offer answers with the qualifier that this was your experience and may not be theirs.

The best help you can give the grieving person is the example you are living, demonstrating how to grieve with hope. This person has now joined your "unwanted" club of grief. Help them see how life continues within this new space of grief. Affirm the mixed feelings they have. Acknowledge their need for space and separation from others. Return to previous chapters of this book to reread how to "walk alongside someone in grief." Be aware of your own needs and don't put upon them the added burden of your grief. I have witnessed first-hand someone trying to help lead a grief group, only to monopolize the time for their sharing of their pain. The result was harmful to the other people who were present. The key takeaway is to consider when you may be ready to help others in the grieving process and then give it even more time. Debbie and I schedule "down days" after we counsel other couples; on these days expect to feel your grief in heavier episodes. It is important that we continue meeting our own therapists and counselors as we help others. Self-care (discussed in previous chapters) is essential as you come alongside other people in the grieving process.

We often want the discouragement to be over, so we live as if there is only one path forward: it's "this OR that." However, our capacity to grieve with hope is based upon our faith that God is still good and active. Faith is the ability to live in the "and." It is the acknowledgement of the reality of painful circumstances but also of the truth of God and His ways. Therefore, I live in the discouragement of grieving and the present activity of God. I live with belief and ask God to help my unbelief. Living with a mindset of looking for God allows me to acknowledge this world is not all there is and Jesus has the final say. This is why I live by faith, in the genius of the "and," not allowing my discouragement to insist on one path forward. I overcome discouragement by acknowledging that the grief I still feel is real and grieving with hope, which propels me to turn to the good.

"Turn to good" is not wishful thinking that everything is "ok" or back to normal. The steps you take to overcome discouragement with positive tasks in remembrance of your loved one will help you to expand your capacity to grieve with hope. The good created in the world by these tasks will help you continue to honor the memory of your loved one until you are reunited together in Heaven. Which is what our last chapter will focus upon.

FOR THOSE WALKING ALONGSIDE SOMEONE IN GRIEF

My encouragement to you is to be supportive of the actions the person is taking. They are expanding their capacity to grieve with hope. You may not understand their need to do something, like start a foundation, but be supportive. You will never fully understand their motivation and need to engage in this new activity, so don't assume you know what is best for them. The concern you feel should be measured with action you can take to help them shoulder the burden of work ahead. I am immensely grateful to those who came alongside Debbie and I in the beginning phase of Adam's foundation to give practical advice and financial support. While some questioned the need for a foundation, we knew we could not just sit in our grief, expecting it to go away—as it won't. We had to expand our capacity to grieve with hope. We had to figure out ways for our lives to continue to grow. We needed to turn to good, and the foundation was our outlet of good in honor of Adam's legacy.

There were some friends who were concerned that we were distracted from the grieving process, but they missed the fact that we needed distractions. Grief is all consuming and so is the way forward through the seasons of grieving. If you are walking alongside someone in grief, help that person to find moments of distraction by turning their attention to God's good activity. Be sensitive of how you recommend new activities or point out new signs of goodness. Allow the grieving person to suggest distractions and then join them in that experience, as this way you will both give support and will be able to sense when the distraction is becoming too consuming. Before you caution someone against a new activity, prayerfully check your concerns with God's Spirit, asking for discernment from other people as well. Ensure the new activity is balanced with the continued previous work of counseling and self-care. Don't add to their discouragement but come alongside them in faith, highlighting God is still active around them.

CHAPTER 14
WAITING PATIENTLY FOR OUR HOPE OF HEAVEN

Pre–June 2022, I lived as if Heaven can wait. I loved this world and all that God was doing in and around me. Now that the turbulent teenage years were behind us, my relationship with Adam was never better. I was a proud papa of one granddaughter and about to welcome my second with Adam's daughter's birth approaching. Our family was close. We were blessed. I believe these reasons created within me a sense of longing for the present and I had little time to wrestle with questions of the "after life." I simply took the reality of

Heaven as a matter of fact. Heaven had little impact on my daily decisions. Waiting for Heaven was something I had no problem doing—all that changed with Adam's death. For the first time, I had questions about what happens after death.

Debbie's Journey

I have a memory of thinking of Heaven often, especially when my maternal grandmother passed away when I was nine years old. She was the first person I knew who had died. In my observing of how my mother grieved her mother, I felt a bit confused. This was the beginning of grief and how I would probably grieve loss in the future. Learning about Heaven in church as a child was always positive and dreamy. As I learned more about God in my own studies as I grew, I did recognize that eternity was where I want to be because God was sending His son to save me. My mother spoke often about wanting to be with Jesus sooner rather than later. She was ill for the last 20 years of her life and would regularly tell me she looked forward to the day she would no longer be sick and in pain. She passed away almost 2 years after Adam. I believe his death sped up her process. With many friends and family members passing before me, I have had more yearning for Jesus to return. I dream of being in the arms of Jesus! I sing the "Hymn of Heaven" by Phil Wickham on a weekly basis for my own personal enjoyment when I cry out to my Savior. In my waves of grief that feel overwhelming I run to His Word every time looking to the hope He gives me, looking forward to eternity in Heaven with Him (1 Peter 5:10). This is encouraging me right now. Jesus COME!

Every civilization in human history has a belief in some form of eternal existence, that we will be somewhere after we die. The Australian Aborigines pictured "The Land of the Dead" or "Land to the West," based upon beliefs that spirits of the deceased traveled west to enter the heavens.[64] The early Finnish people are traveling across a dark river to a water-surrounded realm called Tuonela.[65] In the pyramids of Egypt, the embalmed bodies had maps and money placed beside them to guide them in the future world.[66] The Native American tribe, Cheyenne, and other Native American Plains cultures believed their spirits would join the spirit world and continue to hunt, including the spirits of buffalo.[67] The Romans adopted the Greek mythology of the Elysian Fields as a paradise for heroes favored by the gods or, later, for the blessed dead. Some thought the Roman warriors would picnic in the Elysian fields while their horses grazed nearby.[68] I especially like these last two ideas because they believe in an afterlife where we will be doing what we already know and with whom we love to be doing those activities with. These concepts of eternal life are just human ideas and wishful thinking. Christianity offers the only source of information about the afterlife from One who has been there and gives us reliable eyewitness testimony.

---

[64] Philip Clarke, "An Overview of Australian Aboriginal Ethnoastronomy," *University of Texas Press,* Vol XXI, 2008, 41.

[65] "Afterlife," (2008), https://www.taivaannaula.org/2008/08/28/what-happens-after/.

[66] Richard Sheposh, "Ancient Egyptian Funerary Practices," *EBSCO Knowledge Advantage* (2024), https://www.ebsco.com/research-starters/religion-and-philosophy/ancient-egyptian-funerary-practices.

[67] Joshua J. Mark, "Cheyenne Afterlife," *World History Encyclopedia* (2024), https://www.worldhistory.org/article/2462/cheyenne-afterlife/.

[68] Flavia Claudia, "Roman Beliefs About the Afterlife," *Nova Roma.* Retrieved from http://www.novaroma.org/religio_romana/afterlife.html.

If we honestly consider the weight of our beliefs about what happens to us after death, those thoughts should impact how we live now as well as reduce our fear of what is to come after this life is over. The early Christians had a joyous approach to death and the afterlife. A Greek philosopher named Aristides wrote in A.D. 125, explaining the appeal of Christianity: "If any righteous man among the Christians passes from this world, they rejoice and offer thanks to God, and they escort his body with songs and thanksgiving as if he were setting out from one place to another nearby."[69] However, I had never thought seriously about Heaven, apart from a lecture on our eternal destination in seminary. To be honest, even as a pastor, I had a cartoonish view of Heaven. I pictured clouds, angels, and an endless worship service—which did not excite me. I was living for this world and had no understanding of all Jesus was preparing for me (John 14:3). I realized after Adam's passing that I needed clarity on my final destination. More urgently, I desperately wanted to know what Adam was experiencing. My grief was both the motivation and the limitation of my seeking insight into what Heaven would be. How could I get excited about where Adam was when I was grieving that he was no longer here with me? The problem was I never took the time to discover how much the Bible says of what life after death will be. After Adam died, I took two months to read Scripture and books on Heaven and emerged from that study excited about all that we have to look forward to. The reality of Heaven changed me!

---

[69] Aristides, *Apology*, 15.

LIVING IN THE SHADOW OF HEAVEN

The doctrine of Heaven is probably one of the most underemphasized doctrines of the Christian faith, and therefore many Christians have no appreciation for it. For many believers, Heaven is simply the "P.S." to the Christian life. But we ignore the topic of Heaven at our own detriment. How can we get excited about something that we have no tangible understanding of. Randy Alcorn, in his amazing book *Heaven* said, "We cannot anticipate or desire what we cannot imagine."[70] When Heaven is thought of in metaphorical or symbolic terms, it does not create anticipation within us of a preferred future, it scares us into holding onto our present.

I have come to understand that living here on earth in the reality of Heaven is like playing with shadows on the wall. My oldest granddaughter Ava and I love to play with light and its byproduct of making shadows on the wall. We sit in her bedroom, turn off the lights, and use her night light to create images on the wall. I use my hands to make these animal shapes and Ava jumps to try to "capture" the shadow animal. The shadow game can last for a long time but eventually we get tired of the shadow and decide to exchange the untouchable for playing outside on a swing set that could hold us firmly in the fun moment. This is an analogy for me of what you and I are enduring now: the potential of eternal life is seen, and we interact with it, but the fullness of what awaits us is so much better that we get tired of participating in what are shadows at best of the glory of Heaven.

When you understand the answer to "What is Heaven like?" this knowledge and promise of Heaven empowers Christians to endure grief, suffering, and hardship. If you take this perspective into your

[70] Randy Alcorn, *Heaven* (Tyndale publishing, 2004), 16. Used by permission.

reading of the New Testament, you will see throughout Paul's, John's, and Peter's writings to the early church is a call to endure suffering because of the goodness of Heaven that awaits us after death in this physical world.

> *For our light and momentary troubles are achieving for us an eternal glory that far outweighs them all. So we fix our eyes not on what is seen, but on what is unseen, since what is seen is temporary, but what is unseen is eternal* (2 Corinthians 4:17–18, NIV).

> *And the God of all grace, who called you to his eternal glory in Christ, after you have suffered a little while, will himself restore you and make you strong, firm and steadfast* (1 Peter 5:10, NIV).

Jesus directly warned His disciples to anticipate the suffering they would experience for following Him. "I have told you these things, so that in me you may have peace. In this world you will have trouble. But take heart! I have overcome the world" (John 16:33, NIV). The promised reward of Heaven is both a comfort and a reminder that despite earthly troubles, there is peace and ultimate victory in Him. The reality of Heaven is meant to motivate our faithfulness to Jesus the same way a child might endure an unpleasant dinner for the promise of dessert.

In fact, Scripture commands this should be our focus. "But our citizenship is in heaven. And we eagerly await a Savior from there, the Lord Jesus Christ, who, by the power that enables him to bring everything under his control, will transform our lowly bodies so that they will be like his glorious body" (Philippians 3:20–21, NIV). Paul was excited about the citizenship status Christians enjoy. As much as the Philippian people appreciated their Roman citizenship, the early Christians could rejoice they also belonged to a heavenly country to come. That reality changes how we are to live. Instead of living by the rules and norms of this world, we fix our eyes on Jesus and our transformation that will happen in Heaven.

WHAT IS HEAVEN LIKE?

Heaven can be thought of in the terms of "now and not yet." The now of Heaven exists as a real, tangible place and able to be experienced in ways we know today. In a true "death bed" confession, the thief said, "Jesus, remember me when you come into your kingdom. Jesus answered him, "Truly I tell you, today you will be with me in paradise" (Luke 23:42–43, NIV). The word paradise comes from the Persian word meaning "a walled park" or "enclosed garden."[71] It was used to describe the great walled garden of the Persian king Cyrus' royal palaces. Paradise was not generally understood as mere allegory, with a metaphorical or spiritual meaning but as an actual place where God and His people lived together, surrounded by physical beauty, enjoying great pleasures and happiness. Some theologians consider prior to the resurrection of Jesus, the paradise where Jesus would meet the thief on the cross was not Heaven, but the "bosom of Abraham" where the poor man, Lazarus, was comforted after his death. It is interpreted to be the place of the righteous dead in *Sheol*, but not Heaven since Jesus had not yet provided atonement for sin. However, after Jesus' resurrection, all believers who die go directly to this present Heaven.

---

[71] Strong's Lexicon, "G3857 – *paradeisos*," https://www.blueletterbible.org/lexicon/g3857/kjv/tr/0-1/.

When a Christian dies, he or she enters the place we will call "present Heaven," living in comfort, joy, and rich relationships! The present Heaven will be our temporary dwelling after death. This temporary dwelling should not be thought of as a "less than" version of Heaven. Second Corinthians 5:6–8 promises that when a person dies and leaves their physical body, they are immediately present with God, i.e., what we think of as Heaven. The promised eternal life after death takes us to this glorious destination to commune with God and others (Revelation 6:9–11), however it is not our final destination. My daughter and granddaughter were visiting Debbie and I recently in California. When they flew home, they traveled from Orange County to Atlanta, with a layover in Denver. When we checked them in at the airport, we said they are flying to Atlanta, not Denver. The layover was an important detail but not the most important detail. The most important focus of eternal life is the New Heavens and New Earth, which is our final destination. Our layover after death is the present Heaven until God brings us in the New Heavens and New Earth that is best understood as a resurrected Eden.

OUR FINAL DESTINATION IS A RESURRECTED EDEN

Scripture describes Earth, and all that we know, as a shadow of Heaven; Heaven is the true source material (Hebrews 8:5). So, what exists in one realm (earth), exists in at least some form in the other. Randy Alcorn states: "We should stop thinking of Heaven and Earth as opposites and instead view them as overlapping circles that share certain commonalities."[72] The New Heaven and New Earth will be all

---

[72] Randy Alcorn, "Heaven as Substance, Earth as Shadow," Eternal Perspective Ministries, https://www.epm.org/resources/2021/May/31/heaven-substance-earth-shadow/.

that God originally intended and designed for His original Garden. The restoration of Eden was long prophesied in the Old Testament. "For the Lord comforts Zion; he comforts all her waste places and makes her wilderness like Eden, her desert like the garden of the Lord; joy and gladness will be found in her, thanksgiving and the voice of song" (Isaiah 51:3, ESV). Life in eternity on the New Earth will be a restoration of all things, involving the removal of every impurity and the retaining of all that is holy and good. To be honest, I find it very challenging to walk around this world and imagine it fully restored, with no pollution or decay. As beautiful as southern California is at the beach, I see the litter of trash and broken people all around me. But God promises us something renewed and full of life; that's what Heaven will be like—living in resurrected Eden. We see in Scripture that the Garden of Eden is recast as this beautiful image of a grand city, coming to end this age of sin and death by redeeming all human history in a restored creation. God's space and human space completely overlap again in the final book of the Bible: Revelation. Specifically, chapter 21.

Prior to this final section of the book of Revelation, Jesus, once and for all, destroys the forces of spiritual evil and sends all those who do not want to participate in God's kingdom to a place described by Jesus as a place of eternal torment, it is a place of utter darkness and a place of weeping and gnashing of teeth. In contrast, the New Heaven and New Earth are the promised reward for those forgiven by Jesus. "Then I saw 'a new heaven and a new earth,' for the first heaven and the first earth had passed away, and there was no longer any sea" (Revelation 21:1, NIV). The ancient Greek word translated new here means "new in quality," "superior in character," "fresh."[73] In this context it doesn't mean "recent" or "new in time." Instead, Scripture teaches us (Revelation 21:1 and 2 Peter 3:10) that the world will be transformed into something better; transformed not eliminated. When John said the present earth and heavens will pass away, we should think of the transformation that a caterpillar experiences as it becomes a butterfly; while the former is gone, there is a continuity to the new reality that is.[74] What once was in the original design of earth will be present in the "new earth," resurrected from the curse of sin. One change that will be gone forever with no continuity to the forever Heaven is there will be "no more sea." This sounds terrible for us who love the ocean, but to the Jewish mind, the sea was a place of separation and evil. Our final destination has no evil or separation from God in it, for it will be the City of God.

OUR FINAL DESTINATION IS THE CITY OF GOD (REVELATION 21)

What we think of as the heaven we will spend eternity in, is this New Jerusalem. The City of God is the dwelling of God with Humanity. "I saw the Holy City, the new Jerusalem, coming down out of heaven from God, prepared as a bride beautifully dressed for her husband" (Revelation 21:2, NIV). This is the Jerusalem of hope (Hebrews 12:22) and the place of our real citizenship (Philippians 3:20). Notice the two terms describe this new Jerusalem: "holy" and "city." Holy indicates the purity of this place, different from any current earthly location. However, we know cities. We have specific ideas

---

[73] Strong's Lexicon, "G2537 – *kainos*," https://www.blueletterbible.org/lexicon/g2537/kjv/tr/0-1/.

[74] John Piper, *Future Grace* (Multnomah, 1995), 371, 376.

when it comes to our understanding of this term. Cities have buildings, culture, art, music, goods, and services. Cities are places with many people, and people interacting with each other. Why would we think that when John uses this term it would mean something different? This is the most intriguing description of Heaven I dwell upon. The activity of Heaven will be purposeful and relational and glorious! This is the hope of Heaven!

Abraham looked forward to this City of God, "For he was looking forward to the city that has foundations, whose designer and builder is God" (Hebrews 11:10, ESV). This isn't isolation, but a perfect community of the people of God with God. "And I heard a loud voice from the throne saying, 'Look! God's dwelling place is now among the people, and he will dwell with them. They will be his people, and God himself will be with them and be their God'" (Revelation 21:3, NIV). The greatest aspect of this City of God is God is dwelling with humanity. Coming to a spiritual "full circle" event, God is able to walk with us again in the cool of the day, as He did with Adam and Eve (Genesis 3:8). This restored intimacy between God and humanity is the experienced now as a foretaste because of the forgiveness of our sins. In the New Heaven, what we experience vaguely now will be realized in its fullness. Revelation 21:3 proclaims our new status, "they will be his people, and God himself will be with them as their God" (NIV). This is covenantal language. We will be with God, no longer hindered by our sinful choices or broken lives.

Our final destination of the eternal Heaven is more famous for what it will no longer have: "there will be no more death or mourning or crying or pain…" (Revelation 21:4, NIV). We are reminded of this at every funeral we attend. The movie, "A League Of Their Own," famously gave us the quote "There's no crying in baseball"—which is wrong as I can tell you firsthand the crying I did when I struck out to end our Little League season. The truth is in our resurrected state,

God removes the pain and suffering, wiping away every tear. We are comforted because we are with God. The City of God is distinguished by what it does not have—no tears, no sorrow, no death, or pain. Later it is revealed that the City of God has no temple, no sacrifice, no sun, no moon, no darkness, no sin, and no abomination (Revelation 21:22–23). Why? "The old order of things has passed away… I [Jesus] am making everything new!" (Revelation 21:4–5, NIV). This theme is repeated, four times in the first five verses. What we knew, will no longer be, and we can trust this reality is coming—this is the hope of Heaven.

John proclaims in Revelation 21:9–14 that the City of God is glorious. John was first impressed by the glory of God, as it was expressed in the light shining from the City. This city is very large and brilliant. The length, width, and height are equally 1,500 miles, a cube (Revelation 21:15–21). This is the same distance from upper New York to the Florida Keys; the square footage would approximate the size of the moon. Such a city is too great for us to fully comprehend, and that is the point. John wants to overwhelm us by the splendor of the City of God. Perhaps most famously the eternal Heaven is known for its streets of gold. What we consider so precious now, is simply the pavement of Heaven.

Heaven is a Resurrected Eden, where the City of God is the dwelling of God with a redeemed humanity. Theologian Rene Pache wrote,

> *The emphasis in the present heaven is on* the absence of earth's negatives, *while in the forever heaven it is* the presence of earth's positives, *magnified many times through the power and glory of resurrected bodies and a resurrected*

earth, free at last from sin and shame and all that would hinder both joy and achievement[75] [emphasis added].

What is the nature of our resurrected bodies? Jesus is our example of what to expect. We are promised in 1 John 3:2, "Beloved, we are God's children now, and what we will be has not yet appeared; but we know that when he appears we shall be like him, because we shall see him as he is" (ESV). Jesus looked the same after He arose from the dead and appeared to the disciples (Luke 24:39). This also means ethnic identities will continue (Revelation 5:9; 7:9). Jesus had a physical body—He was not a ghost. When Jesus walked with the two disciples on the road to Emmaus, they did not see anything out of the ordinary, God prevented them from seeing it was Jesus, but they saw a normal man. I take great encouragement that Jesus interacts with His loved ones in His resurrected state: talking, eating, and teaching.

Perhaps our greatest hope of continued relationships is the fact that Jesus' relationships with His disciples continued as they were after the resurrection. Jesus did not have to reintroduce Himself to His best friends. In fact, in an encounter on the shores of Galilee after the resurrection, Peter recognized Jesus immediately after Jesus repeated the miraculous catch of fish that He had done at the beginning of their ministry journey (first recorded in Luke 5). Jesus remembered and was playing upon the relational history He had with Peter when He recommissioned Peter to ministry after a breakfast of fish (John 21). We will even be called by our present names in Heaven, for that is what is written in the Lamb's book of life. We will be known in Heaven as we are on earth—Adam will still be my son Adam. The apostle Paul anticipated his ongoing relationship with the Thessalo-

[75] Alcorn, *Heaven*, 159–160.

nians as part of his heavenly reward. "For what is our hope, our joy, or the crown in which we will glory in the presence of our Lord Jesus when he comes? Is it not you? Indeed, you are our glory and joy" (1 Thessalonians 2:19–20, NIV). As we will still have our memories and identity in Heaven, I believe we will continue to grow in our relationships with our loved ones in Heaven … making up for lost time here on Earth. There are so many topics I want to discuss with my son when we have full knowledge, for we won't have any of our earthly limitations. We will spend eternity experiencing the best of human relationships. This is the hope of Heaven!

HOW DO WE LIVE NOW WAITING FOR OUR FINAL DESTINATION?

> *Brothers and sisters, we do not want you to be uninformed about those who sleep in death, so that you do not grieve like the rest of mankind, who have no hope. For we believe that Jesus died and rose again, and so we believe that God will bring with Jesus those who have fallen asleep in him. According to the Lord's word, we tell you that we who are still alive, who are left until the coming of the Lord, will certainly not precede those who have fallen asleep. For the Lord himself will come down from heaven, with a loud command, with the voice of the archangel and with the trumpet call of God, and the dead in Christ will rise first. After that, we who are still alive and are left will be caught up together with them in the clouds to meet the Lord in the air. And so we will be with the Lord forever. Therefore encourage one another with these words* (1 Thessalonians 4:13–18, NIV).

A fellow professor at Talbot Seminary and friend, Dr. Walt Russel, who lost a son many years before I did, commented this on this passage while teaching a graduate Greek class:

> *While these are certainly rich truths about the end times, this passage suddenly seemed far more oriented to grieving family and friends. It was theology wrapped in real, gritty, painful, emotion-filled experience. It was shaped to address, not an abstract and mechanical interest in the end-times, but the tear-stained eyes of believers who had lost their friends and family members, even their children.*[76]

Paul wrote this Holy Spirit-inspired text so you may not grieve as others do "who have no hope." The reality of Heaven means I can grieve with hope! My hope in Heaven leads me think of friends and family who loved Jesus as they are with Him now: alive, powerful, and active. Billy Graham once said, "Someday you will read or hear that Billy Graham is dead. Don't you believe a word of it! I shall be more alive then than I am now … I will have gone into the presence of God."[77] The great news of the gospel of Jesus Christ is that we wait with hope for the reality of reunion with our loved ones in Heaven. A reunion that will bring us into intimate relationship with God Himself and many others we long to see.

Therefore, we wait for Heaven by setting our hearts on things above, where Christ is. Because we know that Jesus is raised from

[76] Will Parker Anderson, "Celebrating the Legacy of Walt Russell," The Good Book Blog, https://www.biola.edu/blogs/good-book-blog/2022/legacy-of-walt-russell.

[77] Billy Graham, "What Billy Graham Had to Say About His Homegoing," The Billy Graham Library, https://billygrahamlibrary.org/blog-what-billy-graham-had-to-say-about-his-homegoing/.

the dead, then our identification with Him becomes real. It is only because we were raised with Christ, because of our confession of faith in Jesus as Lord and Savior, that we can seek those things which are above. “If then you have been raised with Christ, seek the things that are above, where Christ is, seated at the right hand of God” (Colossians 3:1, ESV). If we really grasp this truth, it will have a profound effect on how we make our choices in “everyday life” on earth. We will make choices based on our hope that we will spend eternity with our holy God and glorified loved ones. When we live in such a way, we store up treasure in Heaven. Jesus tells us of the benefits of this focus as to “store treasures on earth, [is] where moths and vermin destroy, and where thieves break in and steal. But store up for yourselves treasures in heaven, where moths and vermin do not destroy, and where thieves do not break in and steal” (Matthew 6:19–20, NIV, emphasis mine). Remember, if we have stored up treasure in Heaven, we will get to enjoy it there, and that focus will settle our hearts now to live for the reality of Heaven. “For where your treasure is, there your heart will be also” (Matthew 6:21, ESV).

It may be difficult to look forward to spending eternity in Heaven. We don’t have anything to compare to the concept of living eternally in one place, even a place as glorious as Heaven. We live in the “now”—which is like a dot on a page.

Now draw a line going from that dot to the edge of the page. Imagine that line continuing, suspended in time and space, continuing through your house and down the block. The line continues and continues on and on. Living for eternity means to live in the line that continues off the page and into a time and space that we don’t comprehend. We need to stop living for the dot and start living for the line, for that is what it means to live for our hope in Heaven.

Jesus told us to wait for such a time. “Do not marvel at this, for an hour is coming when all who are in the tombs will hear his voice and come out, those who have done good to the resurrection of life, and those who have done evil to the resurrection of judgment" (John 5:28–29, ESV). We wait as we grieve with hope. To grieve with hope is confidence that Martha expressed that she knew her brother Lazarus would rise again at the resurrection in the last day, "I know that he will rise again in the resurrection on the last day" (John 11:24, ESV). Our confidence that we will live forever in Heaven with God is all because of Jesus saying to her, "I am the resurrection and the life. Whoever believes in me, though he dies, yet shall he live, and everyone who lives and believes in me shall never die. Do you believe this?" (John 11:25–26, ESV).

DO YOU BELIEVE THIS?

You were created to be in a good, meaningful, and intimate relationship with God (Genesis 1:26–28; Acts 17:24–27). Do you believe this? However, each of us has rebelled against God's will and reign, asserting our agenda for our lives, resulting in a broken relationship with God (Romans 3:23; 6:23). Do you acknowledge this? The result of living in a broken relationship with God is we are responsible for the consequences of our sinful choices, which destines us for eternal death not the reality of Heaven (Romans 6:23). Do you realize this? The good news is that Jesus Christ came to take our consequences and pay our debt of death with His own life, yet death was not the end of His story, and He arose three days after dying and being buried (Romans 3:24–25). Do you trust this? You can be reunited with Jesus by accepting the gift of His salvation as being enough to restore your life to God (Romans 3:26). Do you believe this? Our restored relationship with God begins as we confess Jesus as Lord of our lives and His resurrection secures our eternal destination of Heaven after our earthly death, surrendering our lives to God's reign (Romans

8:29–30; 10:9–10). Will you live by this truth and place your hope in the reality of Heaven? This is how you are able to grieve with hope.

A FINAL THOUGHT

Expanding your capacity to grieve with hope is ultimately a journey of faith. Faith that death is not the end of our story. Faith that Jesus conquered death through His resurrection and that same resurrecting power lives in me as I have been forgiven and restored into a right relationship with God. Faith that grief has a purpose and that God can still be good and loving to me, even when I don't understand the why of the events He allowed to happen.

Our prayer for you, and those you know who are grieving, is to have peace and joy restored. However, this is easier prayed for than experienced, but we will continue to pray it daily for ourselves, and for you all. Our faith places us in a position of knowing that while we live in the shadow of grief, we wait in hope for the reality of the day when we are reunited with God and our loved ones, and spend eternity in a resurrected Eden, the City of God, our forever Heaven!

> *But Christ has indeed been raised from the dead, the firstfruits of those who have fallen asleep. For since death came through a man, the resurrection of the dead comes also through a man. ... So will it be with the resurrection of the dead. The body that is sown is perishable, it is raised imperishable. ... Therefore, my dear brothers and sisters, stand firm. Let nothing move you. Always give yourselves fully to the work of the Lord, because you know that your labor in the Lord is not in vain* (1 Corinthians 15:20–21, 42, 58, NIV).